Jacob

MEN *of*
CHARACTER

# Jacob

## Following God Without Looking Back

# GENE A. GETZ

Foreword by Howard G. Hendricks

**B&H**
PUBLISHING GROUP

Nashville, Tennessee

© 1996
by Gene A. Getz
All rights reserved
Printed in the United States of America

Published by:
B&H Publishing Group
Nashville, Tennessee

ISBN: 9780805461701

Dewey Decimal Classification: 248.842
Subject Heading: JACOB \ CHRISTIAN LIFE \ MEN—
RELIGIOUS LIFE
Library of Congress Card Catalog Number: 95–40480

Unless otherwise noted, Scripture quotations are from the Holy Bible, New International Version, copyright © 1973, 1978, 1984 by International Bible Society.

**Library of Congress Cataloging-in-Publication Data**
Getz, Gene A.
    Jabob : following God without looking back / Gene A. Getz.
        p. cm. — (Men of character)
    Originally published : When you're confused & uncertain
    Includes bibliographical references.
    ISBN 0-8054-6170-1 (TP)
    1. Jacob (biblical patriarch). 2. Bible. O.T. Genesis—Criticism,
interpretation, etc.   I. Title.  II. Series: Getz, Gene A. Men of character
BS580.J3G48    1996
222'.11092—dc20

95-40480
CIP

7 8 9 10 11 12 13 14 15        11 10 09 08 07

*A*s I've written this *Men of Character* series featuring prominent Old Testament personalities, I've thought about men who have impacted my own life. One of these men is Dr. Howard Hendricks. Howie—as those of us who know him well call him—invited me to come to Dallas Theological Seminary in 1968 to be a fellow professor. At that time, he was going on sabbatical and entrusted his whole department to my care! When he returned the following year, we shared the ministry together for several years until I became a church-planting pastor. But it was the freedom Howie gave me and the trust he placed in me that launched me into a whole new ministry at the local church level. It was also this opportunity that gave me a whole new vision for a written ministry.

Thanks, Howie, for believing in me and sharing your life and ministry with me! You've marked my life. It's a privilege to dedicate this study on Jacob's life to you—a good friend, a brother in Christ, and a fellow professor.

# Contents

# *Foreword*

*I* am profoundly honored that Gene Getz would dedicate this study of Jacob to me. But I have to confess; it's a dubious distinction! For as someone has observed, if Jacob's grandfather Abraham is remembered as a very righteous man, and his father Isaac as a somewhat righteous man, Jacob is largely regarded an unrighteous man. Not exactly the sort you'd want to be associated with!

Oh, he doesn't stand in the rogue's gallery of Scripture with notorious figures like King Saul, King Ahab, and Judas Iscariot. But Jacob was no saint, at least not until God got hold of his life.

Even that took a wrestling match! For you see, Jacob possessed an uncommon amount of that common characteristic, ambition. For most of his life, he was determined to have his way. If necessary, he would lie, cheat, and steal to accomplish that—a "deceiver," his brother called him. Do you know anyone like that?

I do. Some days, all it takes is a quick look in the mirror to realize that Jacob is staring back at me. When I read the biblical account of this man's life, I begin to feel as if someone's been reading my mail! It's extraordinarily personal—and painful.

Yet that's what I love about the Word of God, and why I commend it to your study: it is so refreshingly real! By painting an honest picture of a dishonest man like Jacob—warts and all—God goes to the heart of our human experience. He doesn't play games with us by presenting fairy-tale figures or sanctimonious saints. He shows us life in the raw—and how His grace and power operate in the midst of it.

That's the hopeful outcome of Jacob's story. God did not leave him to his own devices. In His severe mercy, the Lord touched this man in a painful but powerful way that weakened his proud ambition, thereby rescuing his faltering faith. May God touch each one of us in that place of greatest resistance to His will and work in our lives!

I know of no one more competent to lead us in this study than my long-time colleague and friend, Gene Getz. Years ago, I recruited him to work alongside me at Dallas Theological Seminary because I sensed that this man knows what Christian education is all about. I was not disappointed. Gene became known as an outstanding Bible teacher—and something more. He possessed the rare ability not only to explain God's Word, but to engage people in it at their point of need. It's no wonder that God eventually led him into the pastorate, where he has magnificently multiplied his ministry through the many Fellowship Bible Churches that have sprung from his original congregation.

Gene, thank you for writing this book. It draws us back to The Book and its Author, the One whose grace saves us from ourselves.

Howard G. Hendricks
Distinguished Professor
Chairman, Center for Christian Leadership
Dallas, Texas

# A Modern Parable

When I first met Rex, he was nearly forty years old. He was one of those guys who had seen it all and done it all—but suffered the consequences. His problems began early in life. His parents were Christians but had made some really bad judgments over the years. Though they never divorced, they lived separate lives in the same house. They didn't even talk to each other—except when absolutely necessary.

## Two Different Personalities

Rex had a twin brother who was his father's favorite. He was athletic and loved to hunt and fish—an all-around outdoorsman. On the other hand, Rex was more aesthetic and sensitive. He loved to read and write, and he stayed around the house a lot. Consequently, when his father and his brother, Ray, were away on a fishing or hunting trip, Rex spent hours talking with his mom. Needless to say, they became very close—especially since his mother had virtually no relationship with his dad.

Tension eventually developed between Rex and Ray. Being intelligent and shrewd, Rex was able to outsmart his brother. As a result, Ray was always angry because of Rex's manipulation. He made it clear he couldn't stand the sight of his brother; in fact, Ray did everything he could to make Rex's life miserable—even to the point of turning his father against him.

## Off to California

When Rex graduated from high school, he was anxious to leave home. Packing one bag and clearing out his meager savings account, he left for California to make his own way in life. Halfway there he ran out of money—not realizing what it would cost to be on his own.

One day as he was standing beside the road holding a cardboard sign that read "California bound," a man pulled over in a late-model pickup. "I'm only going to the next town," he said, "but you're welcome to ride."

Rex was happy for any help at that moment. He threw his bag in the back of the truck and climbed in the cab. Being exhausted, he soon fell asleep for what seemed to be a brief moment. He was awakened as the driver gently touched him and told him they had arrived at the end of the line. But this man took pity on young Rex and invited him to have lunch in a local restaurant. He then proceeded to share with him something Rex had heard about but never personalized in his life.

"I sense you're on the run," the stranger said. "You seem to be trying to find happiness and fulfillment. I have good news for you."

## An "Angel Unaware"

Rex was suddenly all ears.

"You'll never find rest of soul until you find the peace that God wants to give you."

At that point, Rex knew this man was no ordinary stranger. He really cared! In fact, looking back, Rex has wondered if this could have been an "angel unaware" (Heb. 13:2).

This man—whoever he was—went on to share the gospel message with Rex. He said that we've all sinned and need a Savior, and that's why Jesus Christ died on the cross—to pay for our sins. "He arose again," the stranger said, "and if you put your faith in Him as your Lord and Savior, He'll make you His child. He'll give you eternal life. He is the way, the truth, and the life."

Rex had heard this before, but somehow he never applied it to himself. That day, sitting in a little coffee shop somewhere in New Mexico, he received Christ and was born again.

Though Rex had a new lease on life and a new spring in his step as he continued on his way to California, he soon got caught up in a lifestyle that was fast and loose. He got a job, but in the early years he spent every penny he earned "having fun." He developed friends that were anything but a positive influence on his life. Sadly, he admits now that his next twenty years were more miserable than the years he had spent at home in a dysfunctional family.

However, Rex was an intelligent man. Through sheer determination and manipulation, he climbed the corporate ladder and became an executive in a very profitable company. In spite of his troubled life, he made a lot of money.

It was at this point in his life that I met Rex. He had moved to another city with his live-in girlfriend. He had been offered a new job and was just settling in. By this time, he was twice divorced and had children in several cities.

## God's Providential Care

Some might say our meeting was an accident. Not so! A friend of mine met Rex through business. As they talked, Rex revealed that years ago he had made a profession of faith in Jesus Christ. It also became clear that the woman he was living with was not his wife.

Because Rex seemed to want to talk, my friend called me and asked if I would visit with Rex. That evening, God did a marvelous thing. Rex confessed his sins and asked God to forgive him. Furthermore, his girlfriend also accepted Jesus Christ as her personal Lord and Savior. Together we all knelt and prayed, and they began a new life. After some rather intense counseling, they were married.

I wish I could tell you everything was wonderful for Rex and Carol after that, but they both sensed great responsibility for Rex's children. Rex also decided he needed to meet some legal obligations that resulted from his previous marriages.

## The Natural Consequences of Sin

Since Rex and Carol became Christians they have learned a lot about the law of "reaping and sowing." Though God forgives our sins, He doesn't automatically undo the results of our past failures. Our sins often produce natural consequences that may affect our lives for years—even for generations.

But Rex and Carol have made a new start! They know they're forgiven. They have never wavered in their faith. They also have a "new family"—a body of Christians who love them and are supporting them in prayer as they face the challenges of their past.

In essence, this story is true, but it represents "many stories"—the lives of people to whom I've ministered over the years. And it reflects another story—the life of Jacob.

## God's Marvelous Grace

What you're about to read is the Old Testament account of Jacob—an amazing story of God's grace. He too was a twin. He too left home, running for his life because his brother, Esau, wanted to kill him. But God in His love and grace appeared to Jacob in a dream at Bethel, which led to his own born-again experience.

Unfortunately, Jacob also spent the next twenty years living a very miserable life. Though he married, he ended up with two wives—which was a marital disaster. Though he became a wealthy man, he never attained happiness and fulfillment—until he came back home and made things right with his brother and his father. It was then that he finally took charge of his whole household and became the spiritual leader God intended him to be.

True, we reap what we sow! Jacob experienced that. But God never left him or forsook him. God is still the same today. He will discipline us—not because He wants to punish us but because He loves us. Only God can turn the ashes of our lives into something beautiful.

As you join me in this exciting Old Testament study, I guarantee that at some point along the way, you'll identify with Jacob—or with some other member of his family. But most importantly, you'll discover principles from his life that will help you follow God without looking back!

Chapter 1

# It All Begins at Home
### Read Genesis 25:21–28

God designed the family to get all of us moving in the right direction. It forms the basis of our society. However, when the family doesn't function as God intended, it sets the stage for disintegration in all other social arenas.

The breakdown of the family was a significant factor in the collapse of the Roman Empire. It should not surprise us that the same dynamic is taking place in our American culture. Never before have we had more divorces and single-parent families. Coupled with this trend is the influence of the "Gay Agenda," which denies God's natural plan of procreation and parenting.

Let's face reality. If we don't reverse this trend, it will be just a matter of time before the infrastructure of our own society is so weakened that it will crumble as well.

Is there hope? Yes! There is always hope for Christians—not necessarily to dramatically reverse cultural trends, but rather to be able to rise above these trends and keep our own families from disintegrating with our society. This is why the principles we can learn and apply from these Old Testament examples are so powerful and encouraging. Let's see what we can learn from Jacob's family experience.

## An Unforgettable Moment

Jacob's father, Isaac, certainly knew about God's unconditional promises to his own father, Abraham—that he was initially called to be the one

*[handwritten: Jesus came through the line of Abraham]*

*[handwritten: wow]*

through whom God would carry out His divine plan to bless all people in the world (Gen. 12:1–3). When Isaac was just a young lad, God had imprinted this marvelous truth in his mind on Mount Moriah when He tested Abraham, asking him to offer Isaac as a burnt offering (22:1–2). Isaac could never have forgotten God's intervention. After all, his father's hand was in motion, wielding the knife that seemed destined to snuff out Isaac's life (22:10). In that never-to-be-forgotten moment, God spoke to Abraham—as Isaac listened in—and then provided a sacrificial ram (22:13–14).

Isaac's part in God's great plan is unmistakably clear. We read: "The angel of the Lord called to Abraham from heaven a second time and said, 'I swear by myself, declares the Lord, that because you have done this and have not withheld your son, your only son, I will surely bless you and make your descendants as numerous as the stars in the sky and as the sand on the seashore. Your descendants will take possession of the cities of their enemies, and *through your offspring [Isaac] all nations on earth will be blessed,* because you have obeyed me'" (22:15–18).*

## Isaac's Prayer

Years later, Isaac faced a predicament—in fact, one that was almost *identical* to his father's. Like his mother, Sarah, his own wife, Rebekah, was barren. Nearly sixty years old and after twenty years of marriage, there was little hope that Rebekah was going to conceive. Since Isaac was the promised offspring, how could God's promises be fulfilled?

### A Lesson Well Learned

It was during these periods of anxiety and reflective moments that Isaac did what his father had failed to do. He had learned a valuable lesson from Abraham's mistake. He took the matter directly to the One who had made the promise. He "prayed to the Lord on behalf of his wife" (25:21a).

We're not told how long or how often Isaac prayed for a son. Neither are we told how often Isaac and Rebekah tried to have a son following his prayer. God simply informs us that He answered Isaac's prayer and Rebekah became pregnant (25:21).

---

* Hereafter, italicized words in Scripture quotations indicate the author's emphases.

## Praying in the Will of God

Sometimes God answers a single prayer and does so immediately. Sometimes He responds to persistent and consistent prayers. The important lesson for all of us, however, is that God honors those who pray according to His will (1 John 5:14–15).

Isaac was definitely praying within God's will. God had made it very clear that he would be the channel through whom all nations would be blessed. Furthermore, Isaac didn't want to repeat his father's mistake and try to bring a child into the world through another woman other than his wife. He must have remembered the times his brother Ishmael "pushed and shoved him" and jealously mocked him—which caused a literal separation in the family. How could he forget the angry words from his mother, Sarah, when she screamed at his father, "Get rid of that slave woman and her son, for that slave woman's son will never share in the inheritance with my son Isaac" (Gen. 21:10).

## *Rebekah's Prayer*

Apparently Rebekah also learned some valuable lessons—probably from Isaac. No doubt they had often discussed her husband's family experiences. She had to know the mistake her mother-in-law, Sarah, made in providing her maidservant as a substitute mother in order to "help God along" in bringing the promised child into the world. Rebekah's encounters with Ishmael—either directly or indirectly—and his sons and their hostile behavior (25:18) were constant reminders of what happens when God's children walk out of His will.

## God's Supernatural "Sonogram"

Rebekah learned that she could consult God too. She certainly knew her pregnancy was an answer to Isaac's prayer. Consequently, "she went to inquire of the Lord" when she faced her own personal dilemma. Her pregnancy didn't seem normal (25:22a). Had she lived today, she would have simply consulted her obstetrician and discovered that the unusual movements in her womb were caused by very active twin boys!

The Lord provided Rebekah with far more information than modern medical science could ever reveal. Not only did Rebekah discover that she was carrying twins—a rather traumatic experience for a first-time mother—but she learned some important prophetic truths. "*Two nations* are in your womb," the Lord said, speaking directly to Rebekah.

"*Two peoples* from within you will be separated; one people will be stronger than the other, and the older will serve the younger" (25:23).

## Fraternal "Womb-Mates"

Hearing directly from God must be an awesome experience! Did Rebekah understand what God was really saying? Did Isaac interpret these very specific prophetic words? With all that he experienced and heard from his father and mother in his growing-up days, he surely understood that God was at work carrying out what He had promised so many years before when He had called Abraham out of Ur of the Chaldeans. Naturally, he would have discussed these wonderful promises with Rebekah.

### An "Earth-Colored" Baby

The biblical record simply reports that "when the time came for her [Rebekah] to give birth, there were twin boys in her womb" (25:24)—just as God had foretold and explained. Isaac and Rebekah called their firstborn "Esau"—a name that corresponded to his physical features. Literally, this name means "red," or "earth-colored." Furthermore, Esau's "whole body was like a hairy garment" (25:25). Even today, children are sometimes born with an excessive amount of hair on their bodies, a condition known as "hypertrichosis." Needless to say, Esau was a unique baby and, shall we say, rather "unrefined." Old Testament scholars C. F. Keil and F. Delitzsch go so far as to state that in this instance Esau's hairy body was a sign of "excessive sensual vigor and wildness."[1]

### Prophetic Symbolism

Jacob was born second. He was definitely a fraternal twin, not identical. He came out of the womb "with his hand grasping Esau's heel" (25:26a)—symbolic of the power struggle that would characterize his lifelong relationship with his brother.

This unusual symbolism resulted in a unique name for the second born: "Jacob," which initially had a positive meaning—perhaps "to protect." Later, however, the name came to mean "take by the heel, trip up, to engage in fraud," perhaps like a wrestler making a sly maneuver in order to win a match. It also later came to mean to "usurp" or "deceive." Jacob's initial activity at birth (grasping Esau's heel) seems prophetic of his behavior later in life in his relationship with Esau. In this sense, his parents didn't realize that his name would come to mean something that wasn't complimentary.[2]

## *Natural or Supernatural?*

The events surrounding the birth of these two boys raise some probing questions. Was it purely accidental or a conscious maneuver when Jacob caught hold of Esau's heel? Casual observation, let alone scientific studies, demonstrates that children cannot consciously or physically grasp objects until much further along in their overall development.

Personally, I believe that there is a supernatural dimension to what happened. In fact, it appears that a "power struggle" actually began in the womb when "the babies jostled each other" in Rebekah's womb. This is why Rebekah was so concerned about what was happening. Before these boys were ever born, the Lord's prophetic words were already being fulfilled. After all, God had said—"One people will be stronger than the other, and the older will serve the younger" (25:23b).

### A Divine Mystery

God has often blended the natural and the supernatural. Jesus Christ, of course, is the ultimate example when He was conceived and born as the God-man. Though He grew physically, emotionally, and socially as every normal boy (Luke 2:52), He was directly conceived by the Holy Spirit in Mary's womb (Luke 1:35). He was both the "Son of God" and the "son of man."

Furthermore, when Elizabeth, Mary's barren cousin, both naturally and supernaturally conceived John the Baptist in her old age, she recognized God's divine intervention (Luke 1:25). And when Mary went to visit Elizabeth in her sixth month of pregnancy—just after Jesus had been conceived—the natural and supernatural blended once again when Elizabeth was filled with the Holy Spirit and John the Baptist "leaped in her womb" (Luke 1:41). Here was a child at the end of the second trimester who somehow comprehended that he was in the presence of the Son of God. Humanly speaking, this is unexplainable. But we must remember that with God all things are possible! (Luke 1:37).

## Fetal Tissue or a Living Soul?

Both this Old Testament event involving Esau and Jacob and this New Testament event involving John the Baptist and Jesus have tremendous implications regarding human life existing in the womb. Though supernatural events were definitely involved in this prenatal activity, God still used natural capacities in these unborn babies to cause this communication to take place.

Scientific studies of unborn children are demonstrating more and more that brain activity begins very early after conception takes place. Those who are pro-abortion and pro-choice and who have any respect whatsoever for the biblical record as well as scientific studies, ought to sit up and take notice! I believe the Scriptures teach and medical findings verify that aborting a child anytime after conception is taking human life, which is a direct violation of the will of God. In rare instances it may be justified—for example, to save a mother's life—but these circumstances are exceptional and very rare.

## *The Natural Bent*

Esau and Jacob were different, not only from birth, but from the moment they were conceived.

## An Old Testament "Evil Kneivel"

"Esau became a skillful hunter, a man of the open country" (Gen. 25:27a). As his natural bent unfolded, he became a young man who loved the great outdoors and its wilderness challenges. Today, we would call him a rugged individualist and a "man's man"—a hunter, a fisherman, a camper, a mountain climber, even a daredevil. Had he access to a motorcycle, he probably would have become an Old Testament "Evil Kneivel!"

## A "Mama's Boy"

By contrast, Jacob was a "quiet man, staying among the tents" (25:27b). Compared to Esau, he was definitely more refined. He was a "homebody," and he probably spent far more time in meditation and simply staying at home.

Today, Jacob might be described as intellectual and perhaps as artistic. He probably enjoyed helping around the house (or the tent). Some might even call him a "mama's boy" since he was very close to his mother. However we describe Jacob, he was definitely unique and different from Esau. Though he was a "womb-mate" to Esau, he was uniquely fraternal.

## A Lethal Mistake

*[handwritten margin note: Did Rebekah tell Isaac what the Lord said to her? "Probably Not"]*

In spite of a great beginning, learning from their parents' mistakes and relying on God rather than themselves, Isaac and Rebekah made a terrible mistake once the boys were born. They consistently demonstrated favoritism. Isaac was attracted to Esau, and Rebekah was attracted to Jacob. We read that "Isaac, who had a taste for wild game, loved Esau, but Rebekah loved Jacob" (25:28).

This parental favoritism only added to the problem that already existed between these two boys. The tension that began in the womb and was obvious at birth was fueled by their immature parents. The results were disastrous in these men's lives and in the lives of their families. It created anxiety and sadness in the lives of their parents—as we'll see in future chapters.

But at this point, let's look at what we can learn from this rather dramatic Old Testament story. After all, this is one reason why God recorded these events for us; He wants us to learn valuable lessons from them (1 Cor. 10:11).

### Becoming God's Man Today

*Principles to Live By*

### Principle 1. A great beginning does not guarantee a great ending.

The Bible is filled with many illustrations that verify this principle. Consider Saul, who began his kingly career in Israel as a humble and God-fearing man (1 Sam. 9:21). However, he became a man who was motivated by intense jealousy, and he even stooped to seek guidance from the Witch of Endor (1 Sam. 28:1–25). His life ended in tragedy.

And what about David, Saul's successor? He is identified in Scripture as a "man after God's heart." Who would have predicted his adulterous affair with Bathsheba that led him to commit murder in order to try to hide his sin?

And then there's Solomon, David's son, a man who was identified by God Himself as one of the wisest men who ever lived (1 Kings

3:7–12). Yet, Solomon's life also ended in tragedy. He disobeyed God by marrying women who "turned his heart after other gods" (11:4).

Who are we to think that we will never turn away from God and follow our own sinful thoughts and desires? Let us never forget the words of Paul when he reminded the Corinthians of the reason God has recorded these Old Testament illustrations—both the good and the bad—in complete detail. Paul wrote, "So, if you think you are standing firm, *be careful* that you don't fall!" (1 Cor. 10:12).

*Principle 2. Though God warns about the possibility of failure in our Christian lives, He also makes it clear that we need not make the same mistakes as our spiritual forefathers.*

Living the Christian life is described in Scripture as spiritual warfare. The battleground is filled with "land mines." However, we can "be strong in the Lord and in his mighty power." We can "put on the full armor of God so that" we can take our "stand against the devil's schemes" (Eph. 6:10–11). We need not succumb to Satan's diabolical schemes. Thus Paul wrote:

> Therefore put on the full armor of God, so that when the day of evil comes, you may be able to stand your ground, and after you have done everything, to stand. Stand firm then, with the *belt of truth* buckled around your waist, with the *breastplate of righteousness* in place, and with your feet fitted with the readiness that comes from the *gospel of peace*. In addition to all this, take up the *shield of faith*, with which you can extinguish all the flaming arrows of the evil one. Take the *helmet of salvation* and the *sword of the Spirit*, which is the word of God. And *pray in the Spirit* on all occasions with all kinds of prayers and requests. With this in mind, be alert and always keep on praying for all the saints. (Eph. 6:13–18)

Note too that Paul in the same context in which he warned Christians to "be careful that you don't fall!" went on to write these very encouraging words: "No temptation has seized you except what is common to man. And God is faithful; he will not let you be tempted beyond what you can bear. But when you are tempted, he will also provide a way out so that you can stand up under it (1 Cor. 10:13). These indeed are reassuring words!

*Principle 3. Consistently violating God's will as parents can lead to devastating results in our children's lives—and in their children's lives.*

Parents do many things that can be classified as sin against their children. Writing to the Ephesians, Paul wrote, "Fathers, do not exasperate your children; instead bring them up in the training and instruction of the Lord" (Eph. 6:4). In his letter to the Colossians, Paul stated the same concern a bit differently: "Fathers, do not embitter your children, or they will become discouraged" (Col. 3:21).

Showing favoritism is one of the most serious ways parents violate Paul's parenting principles. This is graphically illustrated by Isaac and Rebekah. And the story of Jacob's life dramatically shows what happens when we sin against our children in this way.

As parents, we must do all we can to treat all of our children equitably. This does not mean we shouldn't reward good behavior, but we must do so in a way that is always fair and just. This calls for a great deal of wisdom. But let us never forget God's promise to all of us: "If any of you lacks wisdom, he should ask God, who gives generously to all without finding fault, and it will be given to him" (James 1:5).

## Personalizing These Principles

Use the following questions to reflect on your own life as a Christian—but particularly as a Christian parent:

1. Have I taken seriously the examples in the Old Testament that vividly illustrate that a good start in my Christian life does not guarantee a great ending? To what extent am I motivated by subtle pride—believing that what happened to them will never happen to me?

2. Do I daily put on God's armor in order to defeat Satan? What about the:
   ☐ Belt of truth?
   ☐ Breastplate of righteousness?
   ☐ Gospel of peace?
   ☐ Shield of faith?
   ☐ Helmet of salvation?
   ☐ Sword of the Spirit?
   ☐ Word of God?
   ☐ All kinds of prayers and requests?

3. As a parent, am I constantly on guard against Satan's schemes, realizing that one of his favorite "flaming arrows" is to cause me to sin against my children by showing favoritism?

## Set a Goal

In view of this personal evaluation, what principles from Jacob's life are you practicing consistently? Conversely, what principles are you violating the most? For example, have you become aware of your tendency toward pride, believing that what has happened to others in terms of spiritual failure will never happen to you? As you discover your particular need, write out a specific goal that you want to reach in order to make necessary changes in your Christian life:

_____

_____

_____

_____

_____

## Memorize the Following Scripture

*For our struggle is not against flesh and blood, but against the rulers, against the authorities, against the powers of this dark world and against the spiritual forces of evil in the heavenly realms. Therefore, put on the full armor of God, so that when the day of evil comes, you may be able to stand your ground, and after you have done everything, to stand.*

EPHESIANS 6:12–13

## Growing Together

Following are several questions for group discussion. Encourage everyone to read this chapter ahead of time. Review the major points when you meet together, and then interact, using the following questions:

1. What ministered the most to you in this particular study?

2. Would you be willing to share with us what principle you feel you're violating the most?

3. In what way can we encourage one another in applying these principles?

4. What particular thing can we pray about? If you feel comfortable, be specific enough so we can pray specifically.

## Chapter 2

# A Tricky Plot
Read Genesis 25:29–34

When parents favor one child over the other—particularly to meet personal needs for themselves—children quickly learn to take advantage of this kind of partiality. They discover how to manipulate each other as well as their parents. Since there was a power struggle between Esau and Jacob early in life—if not before birth—it's not surprising that their conflicts intensified.

Isaac's and Rebekah's prejudice only added to the growing tension between their boys. Unfortunately, these parents were motivated by their own personal needs.

Isaac favored Esau because this son could provide him with wild game (Gen. 25:27–28), and Isaac's appetite for this kind of meat dulled his ability to think and act fairly toward Jacob. On the other hand, Rebekah's needs were more psychological. Her love for Jacob was, no doubt, fueled by his quiet nature and his desire to stay at home (25:27). Jacob's more domestic lifestyle certainly would appeal to most mothers. Consequently, Rebekah favored Jacob over Esau.

## Esau's Sensual Lifestyle

From birth, Esau's natural bent cried out for freedom and spontaneity. He grew up loving wide open space and enjoying the great outdoors. As he matured, he honed his skills as a hunter and often returned home with his prize and shared it with his father, who always relished Esau's kill. Since Esau may have already felt a sense of rejection by God because of His choice of Jacob to be the more important twin in His sovereign plan, his father's attention may have served to build up his wounded ego. Unfortunately, Isaac's favoritism toward Esau also reinforced his tendencies to be a man of the world. He lost his spiritual sensitivities.

## A Man of the World

As Esau grew into manhood, his normal, natural, and God-created personality took on the characteristics of his environment. He met other men who were just as passionate as he and whose lifestyles reflected the culture of their day. Together they lived for the "thrill of the kill"—the hot pursuit and the catch of their prey.

But Esau was also introduced to a life of wild abandonment to his sexual desires. Centuries later, the New Testament author of Hebrews used him as a vivid illustration, warning all his readers—"see that no one is *sexually immoral*, or is *godless* like Esau, who for a single meal sold his inheritance rights as the oldest son" (Heb. 12:16).[1]

The phrase "sexually immoral" comes from the Greek word *pornos* and can be translated "fornicator" or "whoremonger." The term "godless" is *bebelos* which is used to describe a "profane" person—one who is pagan and wicked. This New Testament record and interpretation of Esau's behavior demonstrates that Esau's lifestyle reflected the sinful behavior of the world around him. He loved the world, which the apostle John defined in his first epistle as "the cravings of sinful man, the lust of his eyes and the boasting of what he has and does" (1 John 2:15–16).

## The Seed Snatched Away

Esau grew up void of any spiritual interests and concerns. He rejected his godly heritage that came down to him through his grandfather, Abraham, and his father, Isaac. He had no heart for God. Esau illustrates the person Jesus described in the parable of the sower as one who "hears the message about the kingdom and does not understand it." Consequently, "the evil one comes and snatches away what was sown in his heart (Matt. 13:3–4; 19). The "seed" of God's truth seemingly never took root in Esau's life.

## Out of Sight, Out of Mind

To make matters worse, his father and mother added to Esau's tendency to rebel against God. Isaac favored him and made him feel good about himself. And it appears that Rebekah paid little attention to him. After all, he spent hours—perhaps days—alone in the open fields. Out of sight was to be out of mind. Rebekah was more than satisfied with her relationship with Jacob. He met her emotional needs, probably more so than Isaac—which may have also been a factor in the equation that led to their terribly dysfunctional family life.

## Eli's Wicked Sons

Reading about Esau is a vivid reminder of something that transpired hundreds of years later—after God had delivered the children of Jacob (Israel) from Egypt and revealed His laws from Mount Sinai. Eli served as a priest in Israel, and for the most part obeyed God, worshipped Him, and respected His laws. But he had two sons named Hophni and Phinehas, also priests, who are described as "wicked men" who "had no regard for the Lord" (1 Sam. 2:12).

God had provided for the priests in Israel to eat meat from animal sacrifices while it was being boiled and prepared as an offering to the Lord. However, it had to be obtained in a very specific way (2:13–14). Eli's sons violated these guidelines, and God viewed this behavior as treating His "offering with contempt" (2:17).

Again we see that God never covers up the sins of His chosen people. He explicitly recounts their evil deeds—not to glamorize what they did wrong, but to inform us of what happens to people who purposely walk out of His will. God is warning us to avoid these sins so we won't suffer the same consequences.

Eli's sons not only violated God's sacrificial laws by giving in to their sensuous appetites for meat, but they—like Esau—were immoral. They seduced the women who served at the entrance of the tabernacle (2:22). When Eli heard about their wicked deeds, he warned them about God's judgment on men who do such things. But they "did not listen to their father's rebuke" (2:25). In a sense, they laughed in his face and went right on sinning.

Unfortunately, Eli did not follow through on his warnings and discipline his sons. Though he did not participate personally in their immorality, he ate the meat that his sons took unlawfully from the people's sacrifices. Thus, God warned Eli—"Why do you honor your sons more than me by fattening yourselves on the choice parts of every offering made by my people Israel?" (2:29). Through an unnamed prophet, God pronounced the death of Hophni and Phinehas. They would "both die on the same day" (2:34). And that is exactly what happened.

Eli's two sons *fell in battle* against the Philistines. And when Eli heard that both of his sons were dead and that the ark of God had been captured, he "*fell backward* off his chair" and died (1 Sam. 4:18).

Sadly, because of this tragedy, Eli's pregnant daughter-in-law, the wife of Phinehas, was so traumatized, she went into labor and died in childbirth (5:19–20). Ironically, before she died, she named her son Ichabod, which means "no glory." Her final, chilling words were "the glory has departed from Israel" (5:21–22).

In many respects, Eli's response to Hophni and Phinehas is a distant replay of Isaac's relationship with Esau. We have to allow, of course, that Isaac may have been blinded to what Esau was doing, but it's difficult to imagine that he didn't know. And if he didn't know, as a father, he should have, since he was certainly aware of the worldly environment in which Esau operated. Isaac himself grew up in that environment. Furthermore, Esau's lack of spiritual interest was blatant and open. Everyone knew about his sensuous lifestyle. How could Isaac have missed it? He no doubt knew about it and, like Eli, chose to look the other way.

## *A Sneaky Proposition*

Jacob was very aware of Esau's sensual appetites and actions, and he exploited Esau's weaknesses. He knew that Esau was compulsive and thought only of the moment. Consequently, Jacob had been looking for an opportunity to trap Esau in a moment when his fleshly appetites were excited, and one day that moment arrived. We read: "Once when Jacob was cooking some stew, Esau came in from the open country, famished. He said to Jacob, '*Quick*, let me have some of that red stew! I'm famished!'" (Gen. 25:29).

### A Vulnerable Moment

This was the opportunity Jacob had been looking for, and he quickly seized the moment and took advantage of Esau's compulsive nature. What happened doesn't seem to be an unplanned idea. Jacob certainly had observed this kind of behavior again and again in his brother, and he was waiting for this vulnerable moment. In fact, he may have actually planned the event—knowing the approximate time Esau would return.

Perhaps he cooked the pot of food in a place where he knew neither Isaac nor Rebekah—nor anyone else—would see what he was about to do. We must remember that Jacob's name came to mean "deceiver"—and the trick he was about to pull on Esau was well planned. His response was quick and to the point! "First," he said, "sell me your birthright!" (25:31)

## An Irrational Reaction

Jacob's plan worked! Esau responded to his brother's sneaky proposition just as he had responded on numerous occasions to the "lust of the flesh." His sensual appetite at that moment canceled out any rational thought regarding what his decision would mean in the future. "Look," he said, "I am about to die, . . . What good is the birthright to me?" (25:32).

This irrational, immature, and overreactive response indicates not only Esau's undisciplined life but his overall spiritual status. He had to know that being the eldest, the birthright was his. He knew it meant the greater portion of the inheritance. And because of his father's favoritism towards him, he would have certainly known that Isaac wanted him to have this special blessing. But he also knew that it meant being the spiritual leader of the extended family.

On the other hand, Esau no doubt had heard his parents discuss the revelation God had given Rebekah. Had he simply abandoned the idea he would ever be the one who would fulfill God's promise to his grandfather, Abraham? More likely, Esau just didn't care at that moment. He wanted to satisfy his craving for food—and that's all that mattered.

He had all the earmarks of a compulsive personality. When the urge hit, rationality went out the window. Addictive and compulsive men don't think beyond meeting their sensual needs at any given moment in their lives. If this can happen to a Christian who wants to be a spiritual leader—and it does—what about Esau who seemingly had no spiritual life and goals whatsoever?

## "Let's Make It Official!"

Jacob was mentally prepared—*if* Esau responded. He knew he needed to formalize Esau's response with an official agreement, because once Esau had satisfied his physical need, he would simply deny that the conversation had ever taken place. People who are immoral, abusive, and addictive will also lie whenever it is necessary to protect themselves. Consequently, Jacob said, "Swear to me first." The plan probably worked better than Jacob could ever have imagined. Esau responded and "swore an oath to him, selling his birthright to Jacob" (25:33). Though there doesn't seem to have been other witnesses, this kind of promise was taken very seriously.

## The Deal Is Done

Once the agreement was formalized, Jacob carried out his part of the bargain. He "gave Esau some bread and some lentil stew" (25:34a), and then Esau "ate and drank, and then got up and left" (25:34b). He had satisfied his physical need, but in the process he had "despised his birthright" (25:34c).

Esau's behavior is full of meaning, and substantiates what we have concluded about his pagan lifestyle. He satisfied his hunger without a second thought. Moments later, he simply got up and walked away. How reflective of obsessive-compulsive people! Later, however, Esau would deeply regret his actions when reality hit him full force. That's why the author of Hebrews also stated, "Afterward, as you know, when he [Esau] wanted to inherit this blessing, he was rejected. He could bring about no change of mind, *though he sought the blessing with tears*" (Heb. 12:17).

## Not beyond Hope

It is true that God had chosen Jacob over Esau, even "before the twins were born or had done anything good or bad" (Rom. 9:11). We make choices all the time based on our personal preferences and desires and apart from total objectivity. Shouldn't God have the right to make those same kinds of choices—much more so than we? After all, He *is God!* And His motives are always righteous and holy and fair, which ours certainly are not!

This does not mean that Esau was destined by God to be immoral and godless. These were personal and responsible choices. And the fact that he wept over his decision—even though it was more motivated by his sense of loss than repentance—indicates he still had a soft, responsive heart. Had he cried out to God for forgiveness, God would have responded, for—as Peter reminds us—He does not want "anyone to perish, but everyone [which certainly includes Esau] to come to repentance" (2 Pet. 3:9). Though we in our humanness cannot reconcile God's sovereign choices and our free will, they are reconcilable from God's eternal perspective. This we must simply accept by faith.

## Jacob, Too, Was Wrong!

The facts are that, at this moment in his life, Esau made a rash decision that demonstrated his carnal and fleshly nature. At the same time, Jacob took matters into his own hands and manipulated Esau. Though God had promised and revealed that Jacob would be the heir that He had chosen to reveal the Messiah, it was not proper for Jacob to do what he did. His motives were selfish and, in some respects, just as carnal and sinful as Esau's. He had no right to take advantage of Esau's weaknesses in order to "feather his own nest." And even if he felt he was "helping God out," it was just as wrong as when Sarah tried to "help God out" by providing Abraham with her handmaiden in order to provide a son for her husband. And like Abraham and Sarah, Jacob and the woman he would eventually marry would also suffer the consequences of his sinful actions.

## Becoming God's Man Today

*Principles to Live By*

*Principle 1. All of us must be aware of our human tendencies to allow our fleshly and carnal desires to dominate and control our minds and hearts.*

This is true for both Christians and non-Christians. Knowing Christ personally does not preclude this kind of temptation. Just recently I discovered that a prominent Christian leader has been addicted to pornography since he was an early teenager. Unfortunately, it broke up his marriage, devastated his children, and all but destroyed his ministry opportunities.

For years he has lived a lie and manipulated his wife into covering for him. Rather than face his problem, seek help, and experience the freedom God wanted him to have, he was not willing to let go of this sin. Though it appears he tried on occasions to solve the problem by himself, his efforts always ended in failure.

Many men are subject to addictions of one kind or another—food, material things, alcohol, tobacco, and sexual obsessions and compulsions. God wants to set us free from these addictions and "old flesh" patterns.

The beginning point for every person in being set free is to be "born again"—to come to know Christ personally as Lord and Savior (John 3:3; Titus 3:4–6).

Once we really know who we are in Jesus Christ—that we are new creatures and have an exchanged life, we must continually "renew our minds" in order to live in God's "good, pleasing and perfect will" (Rom. 12:1–2). As Paul reminds us, the battle is won or lost in our minds. Thus he wrote, "Finally, brothers, whatever is true, whatever is noble, whatever is right, whatever is pure, whatever is lovely, whatever is admirable—if anything is excellent or praisewor- thy—think about such things. Whatever you have learned or received or heard from me, or seen in me—put it into practice. And the God of peace will be with you" (Phil. 4:8–9).

*Principle 2. No matter what the circumstances, it is never right or appropriate to take advantage of another person's weaknesses.*

Even though God had planned that Jacob would be the promised seed and heir in order to carry out His divine plan, it did not give Jacob the right to take advantage of his brother's vulnerabilities. How much more so for all of us!

This principle applies to every relationship in life—with our parents, our children, our friends, our neighbors, our employers, our em- ployees, our pastors and spiritual leaders, and our fellow church mem- bers. No one is exempt. We must never cause another person to stumble and fall—including those who do not know Jesus Christ.

Paul spoke to this issue as well in his letter to Titus when he wrote, "Remind the people to be subject to rulers and authorities, to be obedient, to be ready to do whatever is good, to *slander no one*, to be peaceable and considerate, and to show *true humility toward all men*" (Titus 3:1–2).

Paul went on to tell Titus *why* we should behave this way. "At one time," he wrote, "we too were foolish, disobedient, deceived and *enslaved by all kinds of passions and pleasures*. We lived in malice and envy, being hated and hating one another. But when the kindness and love of God our Savior appeared, he saved us, not because of righteous things we had done, but because of his mercy" (Titus 3:3–5a).

*Principle 3. If we take advantage of another person's weaknesses, we'll suffer the consequences.*

How true this proved to be later in Jacob's life. We will reap what we sow. In Jacob's case, what he did frequently came back to haunt him in his future relationships. He too would be manipulated and deceived!

Don't make the mistake of concluding that you're getting by with sin because everything seems to be going well! God's "grace rope" is very long, but eventually you'll reach the end. We *will* reap what we sow. We *will eventually* suffer the consequences. It may even take years, but when it happens, it will be very painful and often disastrous.

## Personalizing These Principles

The following questions will help you apply these principles to your life. Answer them as honestly as you can.

1. In what ways do I allow my old fleshly nature to influence what I do in my relationships with others?

2. When was the last time I took advantage of another person's weaknesses—my wife, my children, my business associates, others?

3. In what ways have I suffered the consequences for taking advantage of other people? If I have not at this point, what may happen?

### Set a Goal

Evaluate your relationships in light of these principles. Give yourself credit where credit is due. Then select one principle that points out a weakness you want to overcome. For example, perhaps you've realized for the first time that you manipulate people by taking advantage of their weaknesses. Set a goal to overcome that problem.

_____

_____

_____

_____

_____

### Memorize the Following Scripture

*Create in me a pure heart, O God, and renew a steadfast spirit within me.*

PSALM 51:10

## Growing Together

Review the principles in this chapter, and then discuss the following questions that are designed for small-group study:

1. Why is this study so relevant to men in business?

2. Would you feel free to share an experience in the workplace where you've been tempted to violate God's will?

3. How do you keep your motives pure—especially if you're in the area of sales?

4. Would you feel free to share your temptations to violate God's will in your family relationships?

5. How has God helped you avoid manipulating people and taking advantage of their weaknesses?

## Chapter 3

# A Beautiful Novella
### Read Genesis 25:19b–20; 24:1–67

$O$ne of the greatest influences in a boy's life is his mother. I've seen this in my own son. Though I tried to stay close to Kenton as he was growing, there was no way I could be involved in his life like his mother. She brought him into the world, gently nursed him, spent time with him during the day while I was at work—and thus became a very important person in his life. In the process, she became a little boy's best friend. He grew up adoring his mother.

Don't misunderstand. I tried to be a good father. But I could not compete with the quality time Elaine and Kenton spent together. But now that he is grown, the relationship has balanced out. I know that he deeply loves and respects me, but when it comes to certain aspects of his life, he'll probably always seek his mother's advice first.

Fortunately, Elaine has been a great mother. She's been a consistent role model. Furthermore, she's always helped him understand my schedule as a busy pastor, explaining that I could not be involved in certain aspects of his life, certainly not as much as I really wanted to be. He understood that—though I must admit, if I had it to do over again, I'd say no to some of the things I said yes to so I could spend more time with my son.

## Rebekah Loved Jacob

Jacob was also close to his mother, Rebekah. And since she was such an important influence in his life, we need to get to know her better. Who was she? Where did she come from? What was her family background? What was she like as a younger woman, both before and after her marriage? And what changes took place in her personality as she grew older?

As we trace the story of Rebekah's life, we'll see that she started out well, but at some point in time she got off track and deliberately walked out of God's will. The biblical record is very clear regarding her deceptive nature.

Again, God wants us to know these details, not to glorify sin or to depress us but to provide a backdrop against which we can take steps to avoid Rebekah's mistakes. God has recorded these events to both exhort and encourage us.

As we've already noted in chapter 1, the story of Jacob's life begins with his godly heritage. We read: "Abraham became the father of Isaac, and Isaac was forty years old when he married Rebekah daughter of Bethuel the Aramean from Paddan Aram and sister of Laban the Aramean" (Gen. 25:19b–20).

Clearly, the focus of this statement is on Rebekah. Her father's name was Bethuel, and she had a brother named Laban.

To understand this succinct but truth-packed reference to Rebekah's family background, we need to look at chapter 24 in Genesis where God expands on this brief historical note. The Holy Spirit has invited us to look in on a very intriguing story regarding Isaac's "long distance" courtship with Rebekah and their eventual marriage. It's a *dramatic novella* involving Abraham, his faithful servant, a beautiful woman, a very cooperative father and mother, and a responsive bridegroom.

## Three Major Concerns

After Sarah died at age 127 (Gen. 23:1), Abraham expressed three major concerns for Isaac:

*First*, he wanted Isaac to marry in order to fulfill God's promise that he would be the father of "a great nation" (24:4; 12:2).

*Second*, he did not want Isaac to marry a pagan Canaanite but rather a woman who worshipped the one true God (24:3–4).

*Third*, Abraham did not want Isaac to leave the land of Canaan and go back to his homeland to look for a wife since it might interfere with God's covenant to give the land of Canaan to him and his descendants

(24:6–7; 12:2; 15:18). Evidently, Abraham was fearful that if Isaac returned to Mesopotamia, he might not return to Canaan.

All of these concerns indicate Abraham's strong desire to do God's will in every respect. He and Sarah had tried to take matters into their own hands earlier in life, and he didn't want to repeat those mistakes. At this point, he had learned that there is an important balance between trusting God's sovereign involvement in our lives and, at the same time, using the human capacities God has given us to make intelligent decisions and to act responsibly.

## Eliezer of Damascus

To secure a wife for Isaac, Abraham looked to his chief servant. Though he is not named in this chapter, he was probably Eliezer of Damascus, a man who had served Abraham for many years. From a human point of view, he was in line to inherit Abraham's entire estate (Gen. 15:2). Of course, when Ishmael and Isaac were born, this possibility no longer existed.

### Loyal

If indeed this servant was Eliezer, we've come face-to-face with a very mature man of God. Knowing he may have inherited all that Abraham had—which was enormous even before the boys were born (13:2)—it is a mark of great spiritual maturity and loyalty for Eliezer to remove those thoughts from his mind and to serve Abraham faithfully and honestly once that prospect was eliminated. As we move through this historical account, we will see this maturity verified.

### Trustworthy

Abraham trusted Eliezer unquestioningly. At the time Abraham charged him to carry out this task, this chief servant was in charge of all that Abraham had (24:2). Later in this story, Eliezer himself reported on the size of his master's estate. "The Lord has blessed my master abundantly," he said, "and he has *become wealthy*. He has given him sheep and cattle, silver and gold, menservants and maidservants, and camels and donkeys" (24:35).

Trusting Eliezer with what was both a natural and supernatural task of securing a wife for Isaac was related to the fact that he had trusted this servant with the awesome responsibility of managing and protecting his riches. Surely Jesus had this man in mind when centuries later He told the parable of the talents. Eliezer illustrates the servant who managed and invested wisely. Consequently, his master was very pleased with his trustworthiness and said, "Well done, good and faithful servant! You have been faithful with a few things; I will put you in charge of many things. Come and share your master's happiness!" (Matt. 25:23).

## Faithful

Eliezer also reflected Abraham's faith in God. Though the Lord had not given Abraham specific details regarding where Eliezer should go and what he would discover when he got there, He had given Abraham sufficient promises and experiences to take this step of faith. In some respects, this was a repeat for Abraham when God called him out of Ur of the Chaldeans to go to a strange land. He didn't know where that land was, but he believed God would lead him there. Looking back at God's faithfulness enabled Abraham to once again trust God. Furthermore, he firmly believed that God would build a great nation through Isaac. After all, He had fulfilled the *land promise*. Would He not fulfill the second promise—that his offspring would become a *great nation*?

When Eliezer raised the legitimate question, "What if the woman is unwilling to come back with me to this land?" (Gen. 24:5), Abraham was quick to respond. He informed his servant that God would work it out. More specifically, Abraham said, God "will send His angel before you so that you can get a wife for my son from there" (24:7b).[1]

Abraham was showing great sensitivity to Eliezer. Though he knew in his heart God would provide Isaac with a wife, he informed his servant that he would release him from the oath he was about to take if indeed the woman God had selected would not return with him. This, of course, put Eliezer at ease, enabling him to take the oath and then, by faith—the faith he had learned from Abraham—to set out for Abraham's former homeland.

Eliezer then "set out for Aram Naharaim" (24:10), a Hebrew phrase meaning "Aram of the two rivers." Charles Pfeiffer and Howard Vos state that "this is the section of northern Mesopotamia around the junction of the rivers Habor and Euphrates, a district also known as Paddan Aram ('the fields of Aram,' Gen. 25:20; 28:2; etc.). This area also included the city of Haran (see map in fig. 1) where Abraham and the patriarchal family stopped on the way to Canaan."[2] Today this area is occupied by modern Iraq.

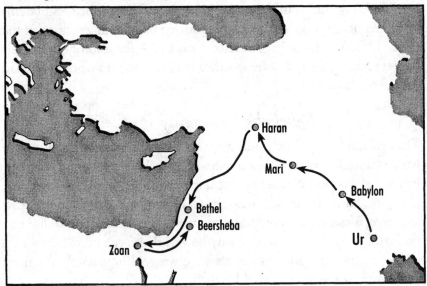

Figure 1

## Abraham's Journey

### Prayerful

When Eliezer reached the town Nahor, which was located in the Haran area and was named after Abraham's brother, he rested his camels and began to pray: "O Lord, God of my master Abraham, give me success today, and show kindness to my master Abraham. See, I am standing beside this spring, and the daughters of the townspeople are coming out to draw water. May it be that when I say to a girl, 'Please let down your jar that I may have a drink,' and she says, 'Drink, and I'll water your camels too'—let her be the one you have chosen for your servant Isaac. By this I will know that you have shown kindness to my master" (24:12–14).

Eliezer's prayer was specific. He wanted a sign from God. And before he even finished his prayer, Rebekah appeared on the scene and fulfilled every specific request Eliezer had just prayed (24:15–21).

Eliezer knew this was God's answer. Rebekah was to be Isaac's future wife. He presented her with gifts and asked about her father—who he was and if he could stay the night. Rebekah's answer only confirmed that God had answered Eliezer's prayer. Rebekah responded, "I am the daughter of Bethuel, the son that Milcah bore to Nahor" (24:24). It's important to note that Nahor was Abraham's brother (24:15).

Following this dramatic answer to prayer, Eliezer once again demonstrated his spiritual character. He "bowed down and worshipped the Lord" (24:26). His heart was filled with praise for leading him to his master's relatives—and more specifically to the woman whom God had chosen for Isaac.

## Rebekah's Personality Profile

The Scriptures very clearly indicate that Rebekah was not just an average woman in terms of her physical traits. She was *"very beautiful"* (24:16a). But Rebekah's beauty was not just skin deep. She was also *morally pure* (24:16b). Furthermore, she reflected an inner beauty by being a *humble* and *unselfish* servant. Though she had never seen Eliezer before and had no earthly idea who he was or why he was there, she quickly saw that he, his attendants, and his camels were weary. Immediately she drew water from the well and cared for them.

Rebekah also reflected an unusual *spirit of hospitality*. She invited Eliezer to stay in her father's home and quickly volunteered "straw and fodder" for his camels. All of these traits, of course, reflected her father's example. He had taught her to be kind and generous towards strangers. Little did she know, of course, what was in store for her. In her graceful innocence, she had passed God's test with flying colors. Of this, there was no doubt in Eliezer's mind!

## Laban's Mixed Motives

It only took moments for Rebekah to run home and report her unusual experiences to her mother and her whole household. Laban, Rebekah's brother, was particularly intrigued, though his motives were certainly materialistic. He was very impressed with the jewelry Eliezer had given her and quickly concluded from the size of Eliezer's entourage that he was representing a very wealthy man. Though he laced his responses to Eliezer with spiritual innuendoes, we'll see in future chapters that Laban was a very shrewd man. To say the least, he had mixed motives when he said, "Come, you who are blessed by the LORD, . . . Why are you standing out here? I have prepared the house and a place for the camels" (24:31).

## *"I Must Talk Before I Eat"*

Eliezer appreciated this generous hospitality. However, before he would touch a morsel of food, he informed them he must talk before he ate (24:33). Laban, who seemed to wield a great deal of authority in the household, asked Eliezer to go ahead and share what was on his mind and in his heart. And thus Eliezer did, reporting in great detail what had happened from the time Abraham had commissioned him to come to his homeland to look for a wife for his son, Isaac. He also proceeded to repeat every detail that had taken place from the time he had arrived in Nahor. It's obvious that he wanted Rebekah's father and brother to be just as certain as he was that Rebekah was the girl for Isaac (24:34–49).

## *"This Is from the Lord!"*

Eliezer's tedious report paid off. We read that "Laban and Bethuel answered, 'This is from the Lord; we can say nothing to you one way or the other. Here is Rebekah; take her and go, and let her become the wife of your master's son, as the Lord has directed'" (24:50–51). Rebekah's father and brother were absolutely convinced that God had orchestrated all that had happened. And, of course, He had!

At this moment, Eliezer once again demonstrated his intimate relationship with God. When he heard what they had said, "He bowed down to the ground before the Lord" (24:52). He then showered Rebekah with more gifts and "also gave costly gifts to her brother and to her mother" (24:53). Laban would have been particularly overjoyed. As we will get to know this man better, we'll see that it's difficult to discern—even at this moment in his life—whether he wanted what was best for his sister or what was best for himself! One way or another, he certainly felt he could "have his cake and eat it too."

## *"I Will Go"*

The next morning, Eliezer was ready to leave. Understandably, he faced some resistance. After all, only a few hours had passed since they first met at the well outside the town. Her family suggested allowing her to have "ten days or so" to get ready to leave her family. However, Eliezer was insistent. He wanted to complete his task as soon as possible and return to Abraham.

Wisely, the family consulted Rebekah. Obviously, she was impressed with all that she had heard. When asked if she would go with Eliezer, she quickly replied—"I will go" (24:57–58). Here we see another quality in Rebekah. Though from a human point of view she was probably excited at the prospect of marriage, she certainly was also very impressed with what had just happened to her. After all, both her words and her actions were a direct fulfillment of Eliezer's specific request of God. How could she deny God's supernatural involvement in this encounter. She *must* submit to God's sovereign will.

Rebekah's family agreed with her decision. They sent her on her way with her maidservants and with her own private nurse. As she and her own entourage were about to mount their camels, her family gave Rebekah a special blessing—one that is very familiar because of its similarities to the promises God gave Abraham: "Our sister, may you increase to thousands upon thousands; may your offspring possess the gates of their enemies" (24:60).

## A Romantic Moment

Imagine what was going through Isaac's mind and heart. He had to wonder if Eliezer had found a girl willing to be his wife. And would he be attracted to her? We can only guess what he was thinking about on the evening he went out into the field "to meditate."[3] It was while he was in this state of mind that "he looked up" and "saw camels approaching."

At that moment, "Rebekah also looked up and saw Isaac"—definitely a romantic moment in God's sovereign plan (24:63–64). Though it would take a while for the distance that separated them to narrow to the point that they could see each other's faces and look into each other's eyes, Rebekah would soon discover that the man who was coming toward her was Isaac—her future husband.

In Middle Eastern fashion, Rebekah "took her veil and covered herself" (24:65). In the meantime, Eliezer reported to Isaac everything that had happened. Isaac too was convinced that this was the girl that God had prepared for him. Consequently, we read: "Isaac brought her into the tent of his mother Sarah, and he married Rebekah. So she became his wife, and he loved her; and Isaac was comforted after his mother's death" (24:67).

## Becoming God's Man Today

*Principles to Live By*

### Principle 1. We should avoid relationships with unbelievers that will inevitably spiritually sidetrack us.

Abraham knew it would be out of the will of God for his son, Isaac, to select a wife from the Canaanite women. They were pagans and idolaters. Even in his day, Abraham understood what Paul taught the Corinthians centuries later: "Do not be yoked together with unbelievers. For what do righteousness and wickedness have in common? Or what fellowship can light have with darkness? What harmony is there between Christ and Belial? What does a believer have in common with an unbeliever?" (2 Cor. 6:14–15).

The week I was researching and writing this chapter, a Christian woman called about her daughter who was in serious trouble. Not too far into the conversation she admitted her own serious mistake when—after her first marriage ended in divorce—she married a non-Christian, an unbeliever. In fact, he denied the existence of God. Because of his worldly influence on her life, she had stopped attending church. She had no one she could really turn to for help, but because I had been her pastor many years before, she called me. Unfortunately, there wasn't much I could do but demonstrate compassion and offer to pray for both her and her daughter—which I certainly did! But, she violated God's will and was now reaping some serious consequences. Paul warned that this would happen when he wrote to the Galatians, "Do not be deceived: God cannot be mocked. A man reaps what he sows" (Gal. 6:7).

Abraham had learned this lesson centuries before Paul penned these words to New Testament Christians—and to us. With his charge to Eliezer, he was indicating he did not want to repeat his mistakes.

### Principle 2. We should be faithful and persistent in doing the will of God.

This is another principle that emerges from Abraham's life story. He is an example for us all, no matter what our failures in the past. And Abraham's faith—in trusting God for salvation as well as trusting Him for the power to live in the will of God—is frequently highlighted in the New Testament, particularly in Hebrews chapter 11:

By faith Abraham, when called to go to a place he would later receive as his inheritance, obeyed and went, even though he did not know where he was going. By faith he made his home in the promised land like a stranger in a foreign country; he lived in tents, as did Isaac and Jacob, who were heirs with him of the same promise. For he was looking forward to the city with foundations, whose architect and builder is God. By faith Abraham, even though he was past age—and Sarah herself was barren—was enabled to become a father because he considered him faithful who had made the promise. And so from this one man, and he as good as dead, came descendants as numerous as the starts in the sky and as countless as the sand on the seashore. (Heb. 11:8–12)

*Principle 3. God has called all of us to be prayerful, loyal, trustworthy, and faithful servants of God and one another.*

Eliezer, Abraham's chief servant, illustrates this important principle for living the Christian life. His loyalty to Abraham and the God he served, his faith, his prayer life, and his commitment to completing the task God gave him all stand out as guidelines for God's people throughout the ages.

We, too, ought to be servants. Our highest calling is to serve God, demonstrating love, loyalty, and faith. We must dedicate ourselves anew to carrying out all His commandments and directives. As Jesus reminded His disciples, to love is to obey (John 15:10).

We are also to "serve one another" (Gal. 5:13). Though we may not be in a servant-master relationship here on earth as Eliezer was with Abraham, we all have relationships with others that call for demonstrating respect, loyalty, and a servant's heart.

Jesus Christ demonstrated this quality in a dramatic way when He washed His disciples' feet. At the same time, He commissioned them—and us—to serve others in the family of God. He asked His disciples, "Do you understand what I have done for you?" Jesus went on to answer His own question: "You call me 'Teacher' and 'Lord,' and rightly so, for that is what I am. Now that I, your Lord and Teacher, have washed your feet, you also should wash one another's feet. I have set you an example that you should do as I have done for you" (John 13:12–15).

## Let's Focus on Rebekah

As we conclude this chapter, let's look carefully at Rebekah—the major focus of our study. She had a great beginning, but as we'll see in our next chapter, she had a very sad ending.

As Rebekah grew older something happened to this beautiful, sensitive, unselfish, and submissive woman. Why did she become deceitful and manipulative? Why did she encourage Jacob to lie to her husband, Isaac? Why did she take matters into her own hands? We'll answer these questions more fully in a future chapter. But at this point in our study, three additional interrelated principles stand out.

*Principle 4. A good home background that provides us with a sense of security, good role models, and an environment for spiritual and emotional growth does not guarantee that we will never depart from doing the will of God.*

I had another experience the week I was working on this chapter. A young woman shared in a small-group setting that she had a great beginning in life—Christian parents and a positive home environment. However, there came a time in her life when she chose to go her own way and walk out of the will of God. She had a great job, a beautiful house, and most of what the world says we need to be happy and successful.

She went on to share that in the process she became prideful and arrogant. In many respects, she believed she could operate without God in her life. And then it happened. She lost it all.

Fortunately, God used this humbling experience to bring this woman back into the center of His will. Today, she is once again experiencing God's blessings and the contentment that comes from a Christ-centered life.

Sadly, Rebekah probably never became the woman she once was. If she did, we'll see that she spent many years suffering the consequences of her sin because of the seriousness of what she had done. Again, Paul's words ring out loud and clear: we do reap what we sow!

*Principle 5. No matter how commendable our home environment and its positive impact on our lives, a new and different environment can cause us to change our values into the opposite of what we've seen modeled and taught.*

Life is filled with many illustrations of what happens when Christians consistently immerse themselves in an environment that is permeated with values that are contrary to God's will. This becomes particularly dangerous when we associate with Christians who are bad examples. Paul dealt with this problem in the Corinthian church. He acknowledged that it is not possible to avoid contacts with people who are living sinful lives. In fact, how can we be "lights" in this world if we remove ourselves from the world? But Paul warns that to associate and to fellowship with people—both Christians and non-Christians—who are living out of the will of God can lead to serious consequences in our own lives (1 Cor. 6:9–11).

### Principle 6. All Christians must be aware of and on guard against bad examples and false teaching.

Negative influences can come from parents, marital partners, children, friends—even Christians—and, of course, the world in which we live. Sadly, some of these bad influences come from men and women who are in the ministry. These are the most dangerous influences of all.

I'm reminded of a close friend who illustrates these interrelated principles. He had a good home background. Furthermore, he attended a strong, Bible-teaching church. He went to seminary and eventually went into the ministry. He was a creative, talented, and dedicated Christian. God used him in remarkable ways to lead people to Christ and to help them mature in their Christian lives.

And then his life began to come unraveled. He developed a close friendship and business relationship with a "Christian" man who was living a double life. Sadly, rather than changing this man's values, my friend became like him. The results destroyed his marriage, family, and ministry. It was very disappointing to those of us who knew him well. In many respects, he was like Rebekah. He had a great beginning, but a sad ending.

## Personalizing These Principles

Use the following questions to reflect on your own life as a Christian.

1. Am I avoiding the temptation to be unequally yoked with unbelievers?

   If you are already married to a non-Christian, the Bible teaches that your marriage is sanctified in God's sight. You must not seek to be released from this relationship because your mate is unsaved. Rather, do all you can to win that marital partner to Christ—not through verbal preaching but through living a Christ-centered life (1 Cor. 7:12–16; 1 Pet. 3:1–7).

2. Am I doing all I can to live a consistent Christian life in the will of God?

According to Paul, the Christian life is like running a race. It takes discipline and perseverance. Listen to his personal testimony: "Not that I have already obtained all this, or have already been made perfect, but I press on to take hold of that for which Christ Jesus took hold of me. Brothers, I do not consider myself yet to have taken hold of it. But one thing I do: forgetting what is behind and straining toward what is ahead, I press on toward the goal to win the prize for which God has called me heavenward in Christ Jesus" (Phil. 3:12–14).

3. Am I following Christ's example to be a servant of God and a servant to my fellow believers?

Again, listen to the Apostle Paul: "Do nothing out of selfish ambition or vain conceit, but in humility consider others better than yourselves. Each of you should look not only to your own interests, but also to the interests of others. Your attitude should be the same as that of Christ Jesus" (Phil. 2:3–5).

4. Am I aware that a good Christian environment does not guarantee I will not fail God if I don't guard against Satan's evil strategies (Eph. 6:11–18)?

5. Am I aware of how subtly a worldly environment can change my values?

6. Am I concerned about the negative influences worldly people can have in my life?

### Set a Goal

As you reflect on these principles, underline those you feel you're applying rather consistently. Then note one principle you need to pay more attention to in living your Christian life. For example, you may have a close friend who is a non-Christian and who is leading you to do things you know are in violation of the will of God. Whatever your need, write out a particular goal to help you be a more faithful Christian:

_____

_____

_____

_____

_____

## Memorize the Following Scripture

*Therefore, I urge you, brothers, in view of God's mercy, to offer your bodies as living sacrifices, holy and pleasing to God—this is your spiritual act of worship. Do not conform any longer to the pattern of this world, but be transformed by the renewing of your mind. Then you will be able to test and approve what God's will is—his good, pleasing and perfect will.*

ROMANS 12:1–2

## Growing Together

Review the principles in this chapter, and then discuss the following questions in your small group:

1. If a Christian is unequally yoked to an unbeliever in marriage, in business, or in some other relationship, how can he handle the situation in a biblical fashion? How have you handled this kind of dilemma?

2. How can we follow Eliezer's example of servanthood and yet not be "doormats," allowing others to take advantage of us?

3. How have you avoided allowing the environment in which you live and work to press you into its mold? How do you handle relationships in that environment?

4. What specific steps can we pray about to encourage you to practice the principles in this chapter?

Chapter 4

# The Great Deception
### Read Genesis 27:1–28:5

*A*s we once again pull the curtain on Jacob's life, his mother, Rebekah, definitely takes center stage. In fact, she conceived the deceptive plan we're about to see unveiled. Jacob initially resisted the idea, although not on moral grounds but for fear of getting caught. The facts are, however, that everyone in Jacob's family was at fault. No one was exempt. Alan Ross succinctly captures this reality when he writes: "God has always provided direction and enablement for His people to carry out their responsibilities in His covenantal program. Unfortunately," he continues, "many simply persist in handling them in their own earthly way, often complicating matters greatly. Genesis 27 gives us a detailed look at an entire family living this way."[1]

The fast-moving events are filled with incredible drama, reflecting the flaws in the lives of some of the most prominent Bible characters. Because of the high drama and rapid scene changes, the story can be presented most effectively in dramatic fashion. Following is this story broken into two acts, with a total of six scenes, three in each act.[2]

### Act I
## *The Fabrication of Deception*
### Genesis 27:1–29

## Prologue
The first three scenes in this story outline in succinct but vivid detail why the deception took place, how it was strategized by Rebekah and

Jacob, and the way the plan was carried out. At this point, let's pull the curtain on the first scene.

## Scene 1. Isaac's "Blind Spot"

> Narrator: When Isaac was old and his eyes were so weak that he could no longer see, he called for Esau his older son.
>
> Isaac: "My son."
>
> Esau: "Here I am."
>
> Isaac: "I am now an old man and don't know the day of my death. Now then, get your weapons—your quiver and bow—and go out to the open country to hunt some wild game for me. Prepare me the kind of tasty food I like and bring it to me to eat, so that I may give you my blessing before I die."

In this first scene (vv. 1–4), Isaac was 137 years old, an old man, especially by today's standards. However, even though he thought he might die, he lived another forty-three years (35:28). But unlike Moses—who at his death at age 120 could see as clearly as when he was a young man (Deut. 34:7)—Isaac's "eyes were so weak that he could no longer see" (Gen. 27:1). Today he would be classified as legally blind.

### Was Isaac Angry?

Isaac had to be aware of the revelation Rebekah received when she was pregnant with the two boys. God had made it clear that "the older will serve the younger" (Gen. 25:23b). Since Esau was the first born, this simply meant that the blessing was to go to Jacob—not Esau. Furthermore, he probably knew that Esau had already sold his birthright to his younger son. Perhaps he was so angry at Jacob's tricky plot against his favorite son that he determined to carry his frustration to the ultimate level of self-deception and try to blatantly ignore God's predetermined plan.

### Was Isaac Driven by His Passion for Good Food?

Though unable to see and failing in physical strength, Isaac had not lost his voracious appetite for wild game. As we've already noted, this was an important factor in his love for Esau and the preferential treatment he gave his eldest son (25:28).

Perhaps this passion for wild game "blinded" him regarding God's will for Jacob. It's amazing what can happen when we begin to rationalize. One sin can lead to another. Look at King David! He stole a man's wife, committed adultery, and—to cover his sin—murdered her husband. Here's a "man after God's heart" who was so self-deceived because of lust that he literally believed that he was above the law of God.

## Was Isaac a Victim of Senility?

Another possibility—but unlikely—is that Isaac had become senile. Perhaps this is the first case of Alzheimer's disease in the Bible. What makes this improbable, however, is that Isaac seems to be in control of his mental faculties throughout this story. Furthermore, had he been weak of mind, the Holy Spirit would have probably inspired Moses, the author of Genesis, to tell us so, just as he told us Isaac was virtually blind.

## Did Isaac Have a Hardened Heart?

My personal opinion is that at this point in his life, Isaac simply chose to ignore God. As he grew older, he "hardened his heart" rather than his arteries. In other words, he deliberately disobeyed.

But how, you say, could he ignore God's provision of a ram when his father, Abraham, was ready to offer him to God as a literal sacrifice? How could he forget God's promise? The answer, of course, is that all of us tend to forget what God has done in our lives—even some of the most dramatic things.

Perhaps this is what happened to Isaac. I think it's a strong possibility—and a great lesson for all of us. The process of time and the influence of the world has a way of blurring and even obliterating the most significant memories—even God's greatest blessings.

## Scene 2. Rebekah's Scheme

Narrator: Now Rebekah was listening as Isaac spoke to his son Esau. When Esau left for the open country to hunt game and bring it back, Rebekah spoke to her son Jacob.

Rebekah: "Look, I overheard your father say to your brother Esau, 'Bring me some game and prepare me some tasty food to eat, so that I may give you my blessing in the presence of the Lord before I die.' Now, my son, listen carefully and do what I tell you: Go out to the flock and bring me two choice young goats, so I can prepare some tasty food for your father, just the way he likes it. Then take it to your father to eat, so that he may give you his blessing before he dies."

Jacob: "But my brother Esau is a hairy man, and I'm a man with smooth skin. What if my father touches me? I would appear to be tricking him and would bring down a curse on myself rather than a blessing."

Rebekah: "My son, let the curse fall on me. Just do what I say; go and get them for me."

Narrator: So Jacob got two choice young goats and brought them to his mother, and she prepared some tasty food, just the way his father liked it. Then Rebekah took the best clothes of Esau her older son, which she had in the house, and put them on her younger son Jacob. She also covered his hands and the smooth part of his neck with the goatskins. Then she handed to her son, Jacob, the food she had made. He took the food to his father.

## A Communication Breakdown

If Isaac's behavior is puzzling, Rebekah's is more so! (vv. 5–17) Why did she have to deceive her husband? Why didn't she simply talk to him, reason with him, remind him of God's revelation to her at the time she was carrying Esau and Jacob in her womb?

Personally, I believe Isaac and Rebekah had stopped communicating with each other years before. From what we've seen earlier, Jacob was very attentive to his mother and was always nearby (25:27). He would naturally become Rebekah's source of security and comfort. As Isaac spent more and more time with Esau, Rebekah would spend more and more time with Jacob. With this kind of communication breakdown, it's understandable—but not excusable—that Rebekah simply decided to take matters into her own hands and "help God out."

Someone might argue that in this culture, women did not discuss these matters with their husbands, especially if it involved a disagreement. This may be true in certain circumstances (1 Pet. 3:6). But we need to remind ourselves that later on in this story, Rebekah had a very direct conversation with Isaac. She didn't hesitate to speak up. Though deceptive in what she said, she minced no words in sharing her feelings about the dangers of Jacob marrying a pagan woman (Gen. 27:46). And, as we'll see, Isaac listened.

## The "Silent Treatment"

This may have also been the culmination of a long-term power struggle. Both Isaac and Rebekah may have been resorting to that age-old tactic we call passive-aggressive behavior. In short, they were giving each other the "silent treatment."

Whatever the dynamic in this relationship, Rebekah determined she had to help God fulfill the prophecy He gave her regarding Jacob. He *must* have Isaac's blessing in order to "be stronger than" Esau (25:23a). Unfortunately, she forgot that God had made it clear to her that He had *decreed* that "the older *will* serve the younger" (25:23b). What God predetermines, He will bring to pass, though He choses to use human beings to carry out His purposes in this world. But He never decrees that people use deceptive and manipulative methods to help Him accomplish His divine plans. Though there are certainly some exceptions, very seldom does God condone the end justifying the means.[3] He is a God of truth and light and "in him there is no darkness at all" (1 John 1:5). What Rebekah did was clearly wrong. She was a bad example and a stumbling block for her son Jacob, and she dishonored her husband with her forthright and deliberate deception.

## "Playing God"

What an opportunity Rebekah missed! Why could she not remember *why* she had received a revelation from God when she was terribly troubled by the "jostling" in her womb? Clearly, she "went to inquire of the Lord" (25:22). Prayer was the key! If she had prayed, would not the God of her husband, Isaac, once again respond to her request? Would He not keep Isaac from making a terrible mistake that would thwart His providential purposes in this world? Rebekah's prayerlessness in this situation only confirms her carnal and nonspiritual attitudes at this time in her life. Adding to this tragedy is the fact that Isaac, who had modeled prayer earlier in his life (25:21), had probably not done so in many years.

Rebekah was determined to carry out her deceptive plan. She was even willing to take a curse on herself if Isaac discovered the plot. Again, we see her commitment to doing things *her way*—not God's way. She was not even willing to listen to Jacob—the son she loved—who hesitated to participate for fear he might be discovered. Her mind was made up. Perhaps she had rationalized to the point that she felt she was above the law of God and could actually break God's commandments in order to help Him carry out His purposes. Somehow she didn't realize that her wrongful thinking and actions would not cancel out Isaac's wrongful thinking and actions.

## Scene 3. The Great Deception

Jacob: "My father."

Isaac: "Yes, my son. Who is it?"

Jacob: "I am Esau your firstborn. I have done as you told me. Please sit up and eat some of my game so that you may give me your blessing."

Isaac: "How did you find it so quickly, my son?"

Jacob: "The LORD your God gave me success."

Isaac: "Come near so I can touch you, my son, to know whether you really are my son Esau or not."

[Jacob comes close and touches Isaac]

Isaac: "The voice is the voice of Jacob, but the hands are the hands of Esau."

[Pauses and touches Jacob, rubbing his arms]
"Are you really my son Esau?"

Jacob: "I am."

Isaac: "My son, bring me some of your game to eat, so that I may give you my blessing."
[Jacob brings food to him and Isaac eats; brings some wine and he drinks]
"Come here, my son, and kiss me."

[ Jacob goes to him and kisses him. Isaac smells Jacob's clothes]
"Ah, the smell of my son is like the smell of a field that the Lord has blessed. May God give you of heaven's dew and of earth's richness—an abundance of grain and new wine. May nations serve you and peoples bow down to you. Be lord over your brothers, and may the sons of your mother bow down to you. May those who curse you be cursed and those who bless you be blessed."

## Sinking Deeper

When Jacob entered his father's bedchamber (vv. 18–29), Isaac was surprised—and suspicious. His *surprise* related to the quickness with which "Esau" had made his kill and prepared the meat. His *suspicion* focused on "Esau's" voice. It sounded like Jacob.

This scene demonstrates the depth to which a man will go once he has started down the wrong path. Jacob actually brought God into his scheme. When questioned about the short time that had elapsed since Esau had been charged to prepare a meal of wild game, his response to Isaac's question certainly borders on blasphemy: "The LORD your God gave me success," he quickly responded.

Isaac was not totally satisfied with this answer, though it appears his suspicious feelings were beginning to dissipate. Even when he touched Jacob, feeling his "hairy arms," he was still not sure. However, Jacob's response that he was indeed Esau convinced his father. He gave Jacob his blessing, believing he was bestowing it on Esau. There's no question that Isaac was acting in a manner contrary to what God had revealed. The content of this blessing on "Esau" was what the Lord had in actuality reserved for Jacob (compare 27:29 with 25:23).

## Deliberate Disobedience

Again, I cannot help but conclude that this was deliberate disobedience. Though Isaac may have convinced himself he was doing the right thing, in God's eyes it was still an act of outright rebellion. This hideous sin was the culmination of a series of small steps away from the Lord. That's the way this kind of sinful behavior happens in the lives of God's children who once walked closely with their heavenly Father.

<u>Act II</u>

### *The Reflection of Deception*
Genesis 27:30–28:5

## Prologue

Deliberate and persistent sin in our lives always brings negative—if not disastrous—results. We reap what we sow (Gal. 6:7). Though it may take time for our plans and schemes to come unraveled and backfire, they surely will in time—and that's what happened in the lives of every member of this Old Testament family. We see this clearly in the next three scenes.

## Scene 1. A World Turned Upside Down

Narrator: After Isaac finished blessing him and Jacob had scarcely left his father's presence, his brother Esau came in from hunting. He too prepared some tasty food and brought it to his father.

Esau: "My father, sit up and eat some of my game, so that you may give me your blessing."

Isaac: "Who are you?"

Esau: "I am your son, your firstborn, Esau."

Isaac: [Trembling violently] "Who was it, then, that hunted game and brought it to me? I ate it just before you came and I blessed him—and indeed he will be blessed!"

Esau: [Bursts out with a bitter cry] "Bless me—me too, my father!"

Isaac: "Your brother came deceitfully and took your blessing."

Esau: "Isn't he rightly named Jacob? He has deceived me these two times: He took my birthright, and now he's taken my blessing!" [Pause] "Haven't you reserved any blessing for me?"

Isaac: "I have made him lord over you and have made all his relatives his servants, and I have sustained him with grain and new wine. So what can I possibly do for you, my son?"

Esau: "Do you have only one blessing, my father? Bless me too, my father!" [Weeping aloud]

Isaac: "Your dwelling will be away from the earth's richness, away from the dew of heaven above. You will live by the sword and you will serve your brother. But when you grow restless, you will throw his yoke from off your neck."

No sooner had Esau returned from his hunt, cooked the meat, and brought it to his father, did Isaac's and Esau's world turn upside down (vv. 30–34). When Isaac recognized his horrible mistake, he literally shook all over. In fact, the Scriptures state that he "trembled violently" (27:33). And Esau realized quickly what had happened and "burst out with a loud and bitter cry!" (27:34). Perhaps his next words are the most haunting and yet the most revealing in terms of Jacob's early life: "Isn't he *rightly named Jacob*?" [deceiver] He cried out in utter despair: "He has deceived me these two times: he took my birthright, and now he's taken my blessing! " (27:36).

Plead as he might for a blessing as well, it had been given to Jacob. In God's sight there was only one blessing. Though God's divine decree was being accomplished in Jacob's life, the sovereign Lord had not decreed that it happen in this way. All four family members had acted out of God's will for years. This was just the final step that led to such disastrous results and human pain.

➤ Both Isaac and Rebekah had shown favoritism.

➤ Esau became an "immoral" and "godless" man (Heb.12:16).

➤ Jacob had already deceived his brother and stolen his birthright (25:29–34).

➤ Rebekah had devised the scheme that led to Jacob's forthright deception.

➤ Isaac was so "blinded" to God's will by his previous acts of disobedience, that he was trapped into believing the ultimate lie!

Sadness and grief hit them all!

## Scene 2. Taking Revenge

Narrator: Esau held a grudge against Jacob because of the blessing his father had given him. He said to himself, "The days of mourning for my father are near; then I will kill my brother Jacob." When Rebekah was told what her older son Esau had said, she sent for her younger son Jacob.

Rebekah: "Your brother Esau is consoling himself with the thought of killing you. Now then, my son, do what I say: Flee at once to my brother Laban in Haran. Stay with him for a while until your brother's fury subsides. When your brother is no longer angry with you and forgets what you did to him, I'll send word for you to come back from there. Why should I lose both of you in one day?"

When robbed of the blessing he wanted so badly, Esau decided to take revenge (vv. 41–45). Rather than acknowledging and accepting the fact that God had chosen Jacob in the first place to inherit the blessing, he determined to kill Jacob. However, out of deference to his father, he decided to postpone the event until his father died. Incidentally, this action on Esau's part once again reveals that he was not beyond redemption. He still had a conscience.

## The Consequence of Sin

Of course, the plot also backfired on Jacob and Rebekah. Through the extended family grapevine, Rebekah heard about Esau's devious plan, and she insisted that Jacob flee and head for her homeland in order to live with her brother, Laban. Thinking Esau would cool off rather quickly and change his mind about taking Jacob's life, she sent Jacob away not realizing she would never see her beloved son again. No doubt she languished in her loneliness for the next twenty years and probably died a brokenhearted woman, suffering the consequences of her sin.

Jacob, too, would suffer because of the separation. But as we'll see in a future chapter, though God did not forsake him, Jacob's greatest trials lay ahead. What he did in deceiving his father and brother would come back to haunt him many times over the next twenty years. He would experience what it really feels like to be deceived by another.

## Scene 3. Another Deceptive Plot

[Rebekah enters Isaac's bedchamber]

Rebekah: "I'm disgusted with living because of these Hittite women. If Jacob takes a wife from among the women of this land, from Hittite women like these, my life will not be worth living."

[Rebekah leaves the room angry and depressed]

Narrator: So Isaac called for Jacob and blessed him and gave him a command.

[Jacob enters scene]

Isaac: "Do not marry a Canaanite woman. Go at once to Paddan Aram, to the house of your mother's father Bethuel. Take a wife for yourself there, from among the daughters of Laban, your mother's brother. May God Almighty bless you and make you fruitful and increase your numbers until you become a community of peoples. May he give you and your descendants the blessing given to Abraham, so that you may take possession of the land where you now live as an alien, the land God gave to Abraham."

[Jacob exits scene]

Narrator: Then Isaac sent Jacob on his way, and he went to Paddan Aram, to Laban son of Bethuel the Aramean, the brother of Rebekah, who was the mother of Jacob and Esau.

## From the Frying Pan into the Fire

As we've already seen, if we do not face our sins and come clean, one deceptive plan often leads to another. In Rebekah's mind, she had to once again deceive Isaac and get him to agree to Jacob's departure. This time she used a theological argument, and she played on Isaac's emotions (27:46–28:5). She knew that Abraham had sent Eliezer, his chief servant, to their homeland to secure a wife for Isaac so he would not marry a pagan woman. Rebekah, of course, was that wife!

Consequently—and ironically—she appealed to Isaac's sense of right and wrong. While violating the very essence of what she was proposing with her own actions, she then followed this theological argument with a "woe is me" tactic. If Jacob married a pagan, she just might kill herself. Though this may be a rather free translation, it captures the feelings she was trying to convey when she, no doubt, feigned tears of sadness combined with disgust.

Though Rebekah once again took matters into her own hands, trying to solve the problem she had created, God used *all* that had transpired in this story to get Isaac's attention. Once again, we see God taking evil actions and using them for good. Isaac called for Jacob and commanded him to never marry a Canaanite woman but to go at once to the very place Eliezer had discovered Jacob's mother. He reiterated the blessing he had already bestowed and "sent Jacob on his way" (28:5).

## Back in Touch with Reality

In the midst of this difficult experience, Isaac evidently regained perspective on God's will. Again he was in touch with reality. Though he never lost his love for Esau, he now saw that he had neglected Jacob and his place in God's predetermined plan. Most importantly, Isaac had to acknowledge that Jacob was God's chosen vessel to carry out the promises that He had made to his father, Abraham, when He called him out of Ur of the Chaldeans (Gen. 12:1–3).

Did Isaac ever discover what Rebekah had done in masterminding this deceptive plot? We're not told. But one thing is sure. If she did not confess to Isaac and seek his forgiveness, she had to live with the results of this secret sin for many years. The emotional pain must have been horrendous, and it was made even worse by her loneliness. Jacob, her beloved son, was gone and would not return in her lifetime!

## Becoming God's Man Today

*Principles to Live By*

**Principle 1. *As the years go by, we must be on guard***
***that we do not forget God's good gifts to us,***
***as well as the good things others do for us.***

The process of time and the influence of the world have a way of blurring and even obliterating the most significant memories—even God's greatest blessings. It's difficult to understand why our memories are so short. But look at the way people forget the good things other people do for them—let alone what God has done. I'm sure you can think of some examples of when this has happened to you. I certainly can!

### There Is a Time to "Look Back!"

I remember several very significant instances where I've helped people to succeed. It was my recommendation that got them a job, or enabled them to get a book published. Or I established a contact with someone who helped them reach their goals. On many other occasions, particularly as a pastor, I helped people in a time of trouble—helped them with a gift of money, counseled their children, or helped to resolve a marital conflict. However, many times it seems they've forgotten. And, of course, silence speaks volumes.

But while reflecting on people I've helped who seem to have forgotten, I am reminded of those who helped me. One is Howard Hendricks, now a Distinguished Professor and Chairman of the Center for Christian Leadership at Dallas Theological Seminary. Howie, as most of us call him, invited me to come to Dallas and be his associate when I was on the faculty at Moody Bible Institute. This position opened up a whole new world of service, including church planting and preparing materials for publications such as the *Men of Character Series*. That's why I dedicated this book to him. This study has given me an opportunity to express appreciation to those God has used to open new doors of ministry, and Howard Hendricks certainly did that for me.

You see, it's easy to walk away and never look back over our shoulder—especially when things are going well and our egos take control. When this happens, all of us tend to forget what God has done in our lives and what other people have done for us—even some of the most dramatic things.

### Think How Paul Must Have Felt!

Paul faced this problem with the Corinthians. He had led them to Christ. He had laid the foundation in their lives through preaching the gospel of Jesus Christ (1 Cor. 3:10–11). But, in their carnal and immature state, some of these people turned against Paul. They virtually forgot his sacrificial ministry in their lives; they even forgot that he refused to take any financial or material support from them during those early days so they would understand that the gospel was free (1 Cor. 9:1–18). Think of the pain this caused Paul when he was actually rejected by these believers as they turned their affections toward Peter or Apollos or someone else (1 Cor. 1:12). Or even more importantly, think of the pain this causes God when His children forget what He has done for them, when they don't remember answers to prayer, when they don't review His Word and His will for their lives. Isaac's short memory and tendency to forget is a lesson for us all.

### Principle 2. *We must daily remind ourselves to consult God in prayer regarding the decisions we make in life.*

Prayerlessness was one of Rebekah's major mistakes. As we've seen, when she was confronted with the problem of Jacob's promised birthright, she took matters into her own hands and tried to work it out in her way. Unfortunately, she also used deceptive and deceitful methodology.

This is what happens to some Christians when they, too, rely on their own worldly wisdom to solve problems. Almost unknowingly, we can shift into attitudes and actions that are out of harmony with God's will. We can compromise and rationalize. We not only fail to pray but to consult God's divine revelation in the Word of God. We have a great advantage over these Old Testament characters in that, in addition to our having access to God's wisdom through prayer (James 1:5), we have the totality of God's *written revelation*—something the patriarchs never saw or experienced. Of all people in this world, those of us who are American Christians are without excuse.

*Principle 3. We must guard our marriages, never allowing communication to break down or barriers to emerge that drive us further and further apart.*

Something happened in Isaac's and Rebekah's marriage. It seems obvious that communication *had* broken down. Whatever the circumstances, we must never allow passive-aggressive behavior to interfere with the oneness that God designed for our marriages. Giving each other the "silent treatment" is never justifiable.

## An Experience Close to Home

When my wife was in her teen years, her father and mother faced some unusual tensions in their marriage. Communication broke down between them. To send messages to each other, they used Elaine as a go-between. She became their "messenger girl": "Tell your father . . ." or "Tell your mother." Needless to say, the experience sensitized my wife to any form of "silent treatment."

I've discovered that if I really want to hurt my wife all I need to do is withdraw and not communicate. Am I ever tempted to do so? Definitely. Most men are. Have I ever yielded to the temptation? Definitely. This was almost natural for me since my father was a very passive person and my mother, by contrast, was aggressive in sharing her frustration. Dad simply clammed up. This is the way he dealt with his emotional pain—and at the same time, retaliated. Frankly, I don't think he really understood these emotional dynamics. Neither did Mom. However, I grew up thinking this was the way a man *should* respond to an assertive woman.

I've learned that this is not a mature way to handle frustration. Furthermore, it is a very insensitive and cruel way to treat my wife, especially in view of her emotional scars from the past. As we've both grown in our communication skills, we've learned how to keep barriers from emerging in our marriage.

## Overcoming Temptation

All married couples tend to allow communication to break down at points along the way in their matrimonial journey. We all develop ways of handling the pain that results.

When we are tempted to withdraw from each other, we must break through that barrier, confess our sins to each other, seek forgiveness, and then open communication to deal with the issues we face. If we have difficulty doing this on our own, we should be humble and brave enough to seek help. It is never the perfect will of God for us to be divorced from each other—legally or pragmatically. Though Isaac and Rebekah never separated, in many respects they were separated because they were both living in their own separate worlds—Rebekah with Jacob and Isaac with Esau. God forbid this should ever happen to Christian couples!

*Principle 4. Once a Christian steps out of the will of God, particularly in terms of being deceptive, it is easy to take the next step to cover his or her sins.*

This clearly happened to both Rebekah and Jacob. The most despicable act of disobedience occurred when Jacob used the Lord to cover his sin by telling his father that God had actually helped him to make a kill in order to provide Isaac with food. To use God to justify our sins (and in this case, for Jacob to cover his sin) is the ultimate in being trapped. It is also the ultimate in dishonoring the One who cleansed us and redeemed us.

I've seen this happen to pastors. Unknown to their congregations, they are living a double life. However, because of their unique ability to communicate and to "put on a good act" in and out of the pulpit, they are able to deceive their way through their hypocritical maze. What makes this kind of behavior terribly evil is that they are using their religion to cover their sins. Like Jacob's actions when he brought "God's help" into his scheme, this borders on blasphemy.

*Principle 5. God is gracious and longsuffering and allows us time to repent and make corrections before He disciplines us.*

Some Christians falsely conclude that God approves of their sin because they seemingly get away with it. Sometimes things even seem to improve. They're more successful and may enjoy life more. However, God will discipline those He loves. The author of Hebrews made this very clear when he wrote, "Endure hardship as discipline; God is treating you as sons. "For what son is not disciplined by his father? If you're not disciplined (and everyone undergoes discipline), then you are illegitimate children and not true sons. . . . Our fathers disciplined us for a little while as they thought best; but God disciplines us for our good, that we may share in his holiness" (Heb. 12:7–8,10).

We must never take God's grace for granted. He is longsuffering and patient. But the time He gives each of us to make changes in our lives will eventually come to an end. In the meantime, He is waiting for us to repent so that we won't have to irreversibly reap what we sow.

*Principle 6. No matter what our failures, God can take the results of our sins and even work those results together for good.*

This is the great promise—and mystery—we have in Romans 8:28: "And we know that in all things God works for the good of those who love him, who have been called according to his purpose."

This, of course, does not eliminate some of the consequences of our sins. What happens in the future depends on the seriousness of what we've done and how it has affected others. Unfortunately, most of what we do that is wrong does affect others. This was certainly true in this Old Testament family. Everyone was desperately hurt through the sins each had committed. This in itself complicated the overall results. Everyone was at fault.

God does not want us to go through life punishing ourselves for sins we've committed. That's why Jesus died on the cross. He paid for every sin. Therefore, we do not have to do penance the rest of our lives. Rather, God wants us to accept forgiveness for sin. Released from that burden, He wants us to move forward—"forgetting what is behind and straining toward what is ahead" (Phil. 3:13). What lies ahead is "the prize for which God has called" each of us "heavenward in Christ Jesus" (3:14).

This was Paul's philosophy, and it should be ours. There were many things Paul could not undo—including his approval of the murder of Stephen. He never forgot how he persecuted many other Christians. But he did not allow this to hold him back in his Christian walk; he moved forward to carry out the will of God. In fact, his greatest motivation seemed to come from the fact that God had forgiven him. That love and forgiveness motivated him to serve Jesus Christ with all his heart (1 Tim. 1:15–16).

## Personalizing These Principles

The following questions will help you apply these principles to your life. Answer them as honestly as you can.

1. When was the last time I took time to say thank you to someone who, perhaps years ago, opened a door of opportunity?

2. How often do I seek God's help in carrying out my daily responsibilities?

3. How effective am I in keeping open lines of communication with my mate, my children, my business associates, and others?

4. Have I made any decisions lately that are deliberately contrary to the will of God?

5. Do I tend to take advantage of God's grace and forgiveness?

6. Am I able to accept God's forgiveness for sins I've committed, or am I trying to atone for my sins?

## Set a Goal

As you reflect on the principles in this chapter, check those you apply regularly in living your Christian life. Then select the one you want to give special attention. For example, you may be deliberately living outside God's will. Perhaps you're being deceitful. Set a specific goal to take corrective action:

_____

_____

_____

_____

## Memorize the Following Scripture

*And we know that in all things God works for the good of those who love him, who have been called according to his purpose.*
ROMANS 8:28

## Growing Together

The following questions are designed for small group discussion:

1. Why is it easy for any one of us to become deceptive?

2. How do you guard against being deceptive?

3. Would you feel free to share an experience where you were deceptive? What happened as a result? How did you correct the situation?

4. How specifically can we pray for each of you in this aspect of your Christian life?

## Chapter 5

# A Born-Again Experience
### Read Genesis 28:10–22

*T*o this point in his life, Jacob knew *about* God, but it's doubtful if he *knew* God personally. Like so many people who are born and reared in a religious environment, Jacob had a "head knowledge" regarding "the God" of his grandfather, Abraham, and of his father, Isaac, but little, if any, "heart knowledge." But things were about to change—not because Jacob was seeking to know God, but because God in His grace reached out to Jacob.

## "Jacob Left Beersheba and Set Out for Haran"

Jacob wasted no time in responding to his father's command to "go at once to Paddan Aram" (Gen. 28:2). He knew that Esau's threats to kill him were not idle words (27:41). He had probably seen the results of his brother's temper many times before. However, this may have been the first time he was the object of such violent hatred.

Imagine the intensity in his gait as he traveled nearly fifty miles the first day (see fig. 2). When the sun disappeared over the western hills, he "stopped for the night," used a stone for a pillow and "lay down to sleep" (28:11).

Years before, when God had led Abraham—first from Ur and then from Haran—into the land of Canaan, this was the very area where Jacob's grandfather had "pitched his tent," "built an altar to the Lord," and "called on the name of the Lord" (Gen. 12:8b). Unfortunately, spiritual issues like these were not in Jacob's thoughts at this moment in his life. In fact, it may have been years since Jacob had last prayed and offered sacrifices to the Lord. These spiritual disciplines had probably long since disappeared from his personal life. Perhaps they had never been truly meaningful to him, even though he had seen his father, Isaac, worship God in this way.

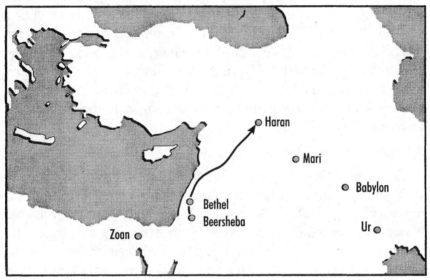

Figure 2
## Jacob's Journey

## *God's Special Place*

To indicate the importance of this "geographical location," Moses, as he recorded this historical event, used the term "place" six times in this relatively brief but very important narrative. This is very clear in the King James translation: "And Jacob went out from Beersheba, and went toward Haran. And he lighted upon a *certain place* . . . ; and he took of the stones of *that place* . . . , and lay down in *that place* to sleep" (28:10–12, KJV). Jumping ahead in the story, we read, "And Jacob awaked out of his sleep, and he said, 'Surely, the Lord is in *this place*; and I knew it not.' And he was afraid, and said, 'How dreadful is *this place*. . . .' *And he called the name of that place Bethel*" (28:16–17, 19, KJV).

It was not an accident in God's overall divine plan that Jacob spent his first night in this unique geographical area. However, it was not the terrain that made this place special—but what was about to happen here.

## God's Special Presence

While Jacob was sleeping, he had a dream, which was no ordinary dream. It was a direct revelation from God—a means that God sometimes used to communicate to people, both believers and non-believers. For example, God spoke to the heathen king, Nebuchadnezzar, and God's servant, Daniel, interpreted those dreams (Dan. 2:1–49). Earlier in biblical history, the Lord spoke to the cupbearer and baker of the king of Egypt with two dreams, and Joseph explained their meaning (Gen. 40:1–23). In the New Testament, the Lord spoke through a vision to a Roman soldier named Cornelius and at the same time spoke to Peter, preparing this apostle to share the gospel with Cornelius (Acts 10:1–48).

### A Stairway to Heaven

There were three important features in Jacob's dream. *First,* Jacob saw a ladder or *stairway.* It was "resting on the earth, with its top reaching to heaven" (Gen. 28:12a). We're not sure what kind of "ladder" this was. No doubt it related to the religious culture of his day. The important thing to note is that it represents "a place where heaven and earth touch, where there is access to God."[1] It reached from where Jacob was on earth to the very presence of God in heaven.

### The Angels of God

The *second* feature involves the "angels of God." They were "ascending and descending" on this ladder (28:12b). It's obvious that God wanted Jacob to know that He was accessible and that He was initiating direct contact with Jacob. The Lord was reaching out to this man who had been living a sinful life—a man who had just a day or two before been a part of a deceitful plot, bringing the wrath of his brother, Esau, down on his head.

### God the Father

The *third* feature in this vision involved *God Himself.* Above the ladder "stood the Lord" (28:13a)—definitely the most important part of this vision. God, in His loving grace, revealed Himself to Jacob. Though Jacob now realized more than ever before that he had a spiritual destiny, he had no idea what all of this involved. Though his father had just reiterated "the blessing of Abraham" as he sent him off to Paddan Aram, Jacob's comprehension of this promise was extremely limited

(28:3–4). Like the apostles who were called by Jesus Christ to build His eternal kingdom, they initially understood this concept in terms of an earthly kingdom and what this would mean to them personally. They had a desire for prestige, power, and material benefits. This is why they argued among themselves regarding who would be the greatest in the kingdom (Luke 9:46–48). James and John, men who were a part of the "inner circle," actually strategized and plotted to set things up so they could sit on either side of "King Jesus" as He ruled and reigned over the nation of Israel (Mark 10:35–37). And Peter's motives were certainly materialistic when he exclaimed at one point, "We have left everything to follow you! What then will there be for us?" (Matt. 19:27).

Jacob, too, did not understand that he was to be a part of building the eternal and spiritual kingdom of God. His focus was purely earthly—involving land, people, possessions, and power over others. Being a "blessing to all nations" and what that meant certainly eluded him. This is why God revealed Himself to Jacob here in this dark and lonely time in his life. As with all of us, God chooses these unique moments when we're often more teachable and ready to listen to His message.

## God's Special Promise

God's presence certainly made this dream an awesome experience for Jacob. It was not only a visual phenomena, but also verbal. Though a dream, Jacob actually heard God speaking.

First, the Lord wanted Jacob to know who He was! Thus, He said, "I am the Lord, the God of your father Abraham and the God of Isaac" (Gen. 28:13b). God then repeated the threefold promise the Lord had given to Abraham involving a land, a nation and a blessing for all mankind.

➤ "I will give you and your descendants the land on which you are lying" (28:13c; also see 12:1; 13:15–17; 15:18–19; 17:8; 35:12).

➤ "Your descendants will be like the dust of the earth, and you will spread out to the west and to the east, to the north and to the south" (28:14a; also see 12:2; 13:16; 15:5; 17:3–7; 22:15–17).

➤ "All peoples on earth will be blessed through you and your offspring" (28:14b; also see 12:3; 22:18).

After God had reviewed His eternal and everlasting covenant, which He had repeated to Abraham on various occasions, He returned to the present crisis in Jacob's life. No doubt filled with fear and anxiety ever since Esau had threatened his life, and having traveled all day long with feelings of despair and loneliness—perhaps wondering if he'd ever see his family again—God gave him a special word of comfort: "I am with you and will watch over you wherever you go, and I will bring you back to this land. I will not leave you until I have done what I have promised you" (28:15).

This must have been reassuring to Jacob, especially in view of his past sins. But something more important is about to happen.

## God's Special Provision

### Personal Salvation

It's my opinion that Jacob was about to experience "justification by faith"—the means whereby we can have a personal relationship with God. To this point in his life, he was in certain respects like his grandfather, Abraham, whom God had called out of paganism in Ur of the Chaldeans and promised the same things He had just promised to Jacob. Furthermore, God had reviewed these promises with Abraham several times (see Scripture references noted on the previous page with each promise). However, it wasn't until years later when Abraham arrived in Canaan and faced the reality of his childlessness that he experienced God's redemptive grace and His provision of personal salvation. God reiterated His promise by reassuring Abraham he would have a son, even though he and Sarah were both beyond the age of childbearing. At that moment, Abraham "believed the Lord, and he credited it to him as righteousness" (Gen. 15:6).

### Peace with God

The apostle Paul beautifully clarified what happened in this dynamic interchange between God and Abraham and how it related and applied to Jacob—and to all of us today:

> Against all hope, Abraham in hope believed and so became the father of many nations, just as it had been said to him, "So shall your offspring be." Without weakening in his faith, he faced the fact that his body was as good as dead—since he was about a hundred years old—and that Sarah's womb was also dead. Yet he did not waver

through unbelief regarding the promise of God, but was strengthened in his faith and gave glory to God, being fully persuaded that God had power to do what he had promised. This is why "it was credited to him as righteousness." The words "it was credited to him" were written not for him alone, but also for us, to whom God will credit righteousness—for us who believe in him who raised Jesus our Lord from the dead. He was delivered over to death for our sins and was raised to life for our justification. Therefore, since we have been justified through faith, we [like Abraham] have peace with God through our Lord Jesus Christ. (Rom. 4:18–5:1)

If my conclusions are accurate, Jacob too is about to experience God's saving and redemptive grace. It was not enough for him to be a "child of promise" and to be reared in a religious environment. It was not enough to know in his head what God had promised. Jacob needed to experience God's redemptive grace in his heart before he could carry out the plans God had designed for him before the foundation of the world.

## *A Personal Encounter with God*

Evidently, Jacob awakened from his dream sometime during the night. Shrouded in darkness, it must have startled him to suddenly open his eyes and peer into the night sky.

### A Visual Similarity

Is it possible that Jacob saw the universe filled with twinkling stars? If so, this experience would certainly have reminded Jacob of what God had promised his grandfather, Abraham, years before, just before his conversion. God took him outside one night and said, "'Look up at the heavens and count the stars—if indeed you can count them. . . . So shall your offspring be'" (Gen. 15:5). It was at that moment that Abraham "believed the Lord, and he credited it to him as righteousness" (15:6). Put another way, this was Abraham's "born-again" experience.

I believe that Jacob, too, was having this same kind of experience. When he awakened that night, the angels that had appeared in his dream were gone. The "words of God" he had perceived so clearly were only a memory. But something had happened to Jacob.

### "Surely the Lord Is in this Place"

Jacob knew that God had revealed Himself. He sensed it, he believed it—and more importantly—he knew God was still present. Consequently, his thoughts were racing. "Surely," he thought to himself, "the LORD is in this place, and I was not aware of it" (28:16). It's one thing to have a dream. It's another thing to know that God has just spoken and that, although omnipresent, God was uniquely present in this particular geographical location. God was speaking directly to Jacob. He was having a *personal* encounter with the Lord.

## "How Awesome Is this Place!"

Realizing what had happened, Jacob "was afraid." Verbalizing his fear, he probably spoke in a subdued but audible voice: "How awesome is this place!" (28:17a). Jacob concluded, "This is none other than the house of God; this is the gate of heaven" (27:17b).

Why did Jacob respond in this way? First of all, the dream in itself was a very emotional experience. I have awakened from an intense dream—as I'm sure you have—with my heart pounding and my adrenaline flowing. However, it has had no spiritual significance whatsoever. It was simply my unconscious mind reconstructing certain events in my life in a bizarre way that created fear and anxiety. What Jacob experienced, however, *did* have spiritual significance. It involved God's eternal plan for all humankind—the plan of redemption and salvation; in short, the "blessing" promised to his grandfather, Abraham. God had just reiterated this promise to him.

## "This Is the Gate of Heaven!"

At this point in time, Jacob did not understand the aspect of his dream in which God promised to bless all peoples of the earth through him. What he did understand was that he had personally encountered a holy God. Against the backdrop of his own sinful and deceitful behavior—the reason he was hurriedly on his way to his mother's homeland—he would certainly become aware of his unworthiness to have received a direct revelation from the God of his fathers.

This is what should happen to any person whose sins have not been covered by the blood of Christ. We too should experience "godly fear"—a fear that drives us to repent, to confess our sins and turn to God for forgiveness. This, I believe, is what happened to Jacob as a result of this awesome experience. He called this great outdoor cathedral "the house of God." More importantly, he identified it as "the gate of heaven."

# A Striking Parallel

When Jesus began His public ministry, He began the process of selecting twelve men whom He later identified as His apostles. One of these men was Philip, who invited his brother, Nathaniel, to come and meet Jesus. Philip made it clear that he believed that he had "found the one Moses wrote about in the Law, and about whom the prophets also wrote—Jesus of Nazareth, the son of Joseph" (John 1:45).

## "Can Any Good Thing Come Out of Nazareth?"

When Nathaniel learned that this man who identified Himself as Jesus Christ was from Nazareth—a smelly fishing village—he was initially skeptical. Since he and Philip lived in Bethsaida, a much more affluent town, he responded with pride and arrogance: "Nazareth! Can anything good come from there?" (John 1:46).

Philip challenged Nathaniel to "come and see." Convinced he ought to at least investigate, Nathaniel followed Philip. But before Nathaniel even had an opportunity to introduce himself, Jesus saw him coming and made a statement that unnerved Nathaniel—"Here is a true Israelite," Jesus said, "in whom there is nothing false." More literally, the New King James reads, "in whom is no deceit" (1:47). Startled, Nathaniel asked Jesus how He knew him. Jesus answered with another stunning statement: "I saw you while you were still under the fig tree before Philip called you" (1:48).

## "Rabbi, You Are the Son of God!"

Nathaniel's response to all of this may be puzzling to the casual reader—especially if we don't correlate this event in his life with what we've just learned about Jacob. Nathaniel turned his back on his prejudice, his arrogance, and his skepticism and unbelief and declared, "Rabbi, you are the Son of God; you are the King of Israel" (1:49).

Jesus' response to Nathaniel's statement of faith helps us read between the lines and fill in the miraculous aspects of this divine encounter between Jesus and Nathaniel: "You shall see greater things than that." Jesus then added, "I tell you the truth, you shall see heaven open, and the angels of God ascending and descending on the Son of Man" (1:50–51).

What was it that happened in this communication between Jesus and Nathaniel that we're not told specifically in John's gospel? Evidently,

Nathaniel was sitting under a fig tree meditating on the Old Testament story we've been studying. He was perhaps amazed that God would reveal Himself in a dream to one so disgustingly deceitful as Jacob. How could a man so sinful be the recipient of God's grace?

Knowing Nathaniel's arrogant and judgmental attitudes towards others—such as people who lived in Nazareth—it would not be surprising that Nathaniel was obsessed with self-satisfying thoughts that he was not deceitful like Jacob. And, indeed he was not, because Jesus identified him as "a true Israelite in whom there is nothing false." Nathaniel was an honest man.

It's apparent that Jesus had read the thoughts of Nathaniel's heart while he sat meditating under the fig tree. He was now interpreting these thoughts, as Jesus often did in His encounters with people.[2] At that moment, Nathaniel knew he was standing face-to-face with the promised Messiah—the seed of Abraham. This was no doubt his moment of conversion—although, he like Jacob, would fail the Lord along his spiritual journey.

## "The Way and the Truth and the Life!"

The most important correlation with Jacob's experience relates to Jesus' statement about "the angels of God ascending and descending on the Son of Man" (John 1:51). Here Jesus identified Himself as the "ladder." He is the "staircase" to God. Later, He made this very clear when He told doubting Thomas that He was "the way and the truth and the life" and that "no one comes to the Father except through Me" (John 14:6).

On another occasion, Jesus used the shepherd, the sheep, and the sheep pen to illustrate the same truth. Jesus identified Himself as "the shepherd" who would lay down His life for the sheep (John 10:11). But with this metaphor Jesus also identified Himself as the "gate" for the sheep (10:7). No one could enter the sheep pen except through Him.

Personally, I believe Jacob's statement was prophetic when he interpreted what he saw in his dream as "the gate of heaven" (Gen. 28:17). In so doing, he was identifying the seed of Abraham—Jesus Christ—who claimed to be the very "stairway" or "ladder" Jacob saw in his dream and that Nathaniel was thinking about under the fig tree. More importantly, Jacob—like his grandfather, Abraham—believed God. By faith, Jacob went through "the gate of heaven"—which, in reality, was Jesus Christ. He is the "way" to God! He "bridged the gap" between humans on earth and God in heaven.

## Faith That Works

As soon as daylight came, Jacob demonstrated his faith with several significant actions. As James wrote: "Faith by itself, if it is not accompanied by action, is dead" (James 2:17). Jacob's response verified his heart had changed.

### Devotion and Worship

Jacob expressed his true heart change immediately. We read: "Early the next morning Jacob took the stone he had placed under his head and set it up as a pillar and poured oil on top of it" (Gen. 28:18).

As soon as it became daylight, Jacob responded to what he knew was God's will. He had much more to learn about God and what He expects from His children. Most importantly, at this moment, Jacob's response was sincere and real. The stone on which he had laid his head that night became an altar pointing to God. The oil he poured on the stone was a specific offering and gift to God. As Alan Ross states, "It was a symbolic ritual act by which Jacob demonstrated his devotion to the Lord and consecrated the spot as holy to him."[3]

Jacob's devotion is also evident in his desire to remember this event all the days of his life, and he wanted others to remember it too. Consequently, he "called that place Bethel," which literally means "house of God." This is where he met God "face-to-face." It was a real experience, even though it happened in a dream.

### Dedication and Commitment

Jacob made his true relationship with God evident with a vow, a commitment. A casual look at his dedicatory comments may appear that his response was conditional; that is, "If God will be with me and will watch over me . . . , then the Lord will be my God" (28:20–21). In other words, "If God blesses me, then I'll serve Him."

To interpret Jacob's response in this way is to misread his words and his heart. Rather, Jacob was simply saying, "If God will help me, I'll fulfill my commitment." In other words, Jacob was acknowledging the fact that he could not do it alone. He needed God's help. God would have to make it possible for him to carry out his commitment.

Alan Ross translates this passage accurately: "If the Lord God is with me and keeps me in this way in which I am going and gives me bread to eat and clothing to wear, so that I return in peace to the house of my father and the Lord becomes my God, then the stone which I set up as a pillar will be the house of God, and all which you give me a tenth I will give you" (28:20–22).[4]

Jacob's vow involved two tangible expressions of his new faith experience.

*First*, he would always worship God at Bethel. He would never fail to remember what happened there. And certainly beyond coming to this place, Jacob was saying that wherever he was, he would worship God, acknowledging who He is.

*Second*, and most tangible of all, he committed to giving a tenth or a tithe to God of all that God gave him. Interestingly, this is what his grandfather, Abraham, did (Gen. 14:17–20). Eventually, tithing became a law in Israel. However, before the Law was ever given, the tithe was a free-will offering in the lives of these Old Testament patriarchs. They were freely responding to God's grace in their lives. God had not even commanded them to give! This commitment, of course, has tremendous implications for Christians today who are living in a materialistic world.

## Becoming God's Man Today

*Principles to Live By*

*Principle 1. All people everywhere—no matter what our family heritage, our religious background, or our righteous or unrighteous acts—need to experience God's redemptive grace in order to "enter the gate of heaven."*

### Salvation Must Be Personal

Jacob was born into a family through whom God chose to bring redemption to the whole world. Yet, he needed to experience that redemption himself. And so did Nathaniel, who was even classified by Jesus as "a true Israelite in whom there is nothing false" (John 1:47). However, both Jacob—"the deceiver"—and Nathaniel—"the honest man"—needed to be saved.

This was the message that Paul was communicating in Romans when he quoted Psalm 14: "There is no one righteous, not even one"

(Rom. 3:10). Having written to both unrighteous Gentiles (Rom. 1) and self-righteous Jews (Rom. 2), he concluded that "*all* have sinned and fall short of the glory of God" (3:23). But the good news is that all of us can be "justified freely by His grace through the redemption that came by Christ Jesus" (3:24).

This is why God chose Abraham out of Ur of the Chaldeans—not just to show favoritism to him, his family, and his descendants, but to provide a national channel through whom the blessings of the Savior might come to all peoples of the earth (Gen. 12:3). When there was not one righteous person on the earth, God, in His mercy and grace, chose one man in order to have mercy on us all.

## The "Father of Us All"

God's grace is indeed available to all people. He does not want "anyone to perish, but everyone to come to repentance" (2 Pet. 3:9). However, only those who respond to God's grace and receive this gift of eternal life will inherit eternal life. When Jesus Christ first came, He came to His own family of people, the nation Israel. But, as a nation they rejected His death and resurrection. They did not receive Him as the promised Messiah. Yet, John recorded that "to all who received him, to those who believed in his name, he gave the right to become children of God" (John 1:11–12).

We must remember that Abraham "is the father of us all," that is, of all who believe. Abraham's faith experience demonstrates salvation by grace through faith. When promised a son in his old age, he "believed the Lord, and he credited it to him as righteousness" (Gen. 15:6). Though he did not understand the full message of the gospel as we can, it was by faith that he looked forward to the death and resurrection of Christ. With the same faith, we look back to Calvary and to an empty tomb. But we are all saved in the same way—by faith. As Paul wrote so clearly and beautifully, "For it is by grace you have been saved, through faith—and this not from yourselves, it is the gift of God—not by works, so that no one can boast" (Eph. 2:8–9). Have you received this wonderful gift of eternal salvation?

*Principle 2. True conversion involves the knowledge of why we need to be saved—specifically, that God is a holy and awesome God, and in ourselves we cannot enter His presence because of our sinful nature.*

When God revealed Himself, Jacob became aware of God's holy presence. Jacob also became aware of his own sinful behavior. This combination created "godly fear."

The way in which Jacob's experience relates to our experience varies, of course, depending on our previous knowledge, our age, our lifestyle, and even our cultural background. However, one thing is necessary: an awareness that we have sinned and fallen short of His glory—His holiness and His righteousness (Rom. 3:23). We must understand that the wages of our sin is death—eternal separation from God—but that God's gift to all who believe is eternal life through Jesus Christ our Lord (Rom. 6:23).

### *"Easy Believism"*

Today we live in an age of what some call "easy believism." Unfortunately, some people "make decisions for Christ" without truly experiencing what it means to be aware of why we really need a Savior. Without a true knowledge of God's holiness and the sin that separates us from Him, it is doubtful that our decision to receive Christ is valid and acceptable to God.

Again, the intensity of this experience depends on our age, previous lifestyle, and religious upbringing. But even children, in their own simple way and at a very early age, can be aware of God's holiness and the fact that they are sinners and need a Savior.

### *We All Need a "Bethel Experience!"*

Can you remember a "Bethel experience" in your own life—a time when you received Christ because you became aware of God's holiness and that your own sinfulness separated you from God? If you cannot, perhaps you need to make sure you really know God personally. Perhaps you've been relying on your parents' faith, your religious upbringing, or on your good works. The Bible teaches us that none of these will suffice. As a songwriter so aptly stated:

> Could my tears forever flow,
> Could my zeal no languor know,
> These for sin could not atone—
> Thou must save, and Thou alone:
> In my hand no price I bring,
> Simply to the cross I cling.

> *Principle 3. Though we are saved not by works but by grace*
> *through faith, Paul quickly and immediately reminds us*
> *that "we are God's workmanship, created in Christ Jesus*
> *to do good works, which God prepared in advance for us to do"*
> *(Eph. 2:10).*

True conversion results in a changed life! We see this in Jacob's experience. He responded immediately to God's revelation. Not only did he experience God personally and "enter the gate of heaven," but he expressed his devotion and dedication to God. He worshiped the Lord. Like the blind man who was healed by Jesus when he discovered that Jesus Christ was indeed the Son of God, and once he truly believed, "he worshiped him" (John 9:38).

## Specific Reflections of Faith

Jacob's faith was also reflected in even more tangible ways. He made a vow or commitment that with God's strength and help, he would continue to worship God and more specifically, to give God a tenth of all his income (Gen. 28:22).

As stated earlier, Jacob's specific commitments have implications for Christians today. How many "believers" truly worship God—both personally and corporately? And how many Christians never make tithing—giving proportionately as God has blessed them—a priority in their lives in order to reflect their thanksgiving to God for His free gift of grace in salvation?

What Jacob did, particularly in terms of giving, is significant because he, along with his grandfather, Abraham, made this kind of giving pattern a part of their lives before it ever became a law in Israel. In so doing, they were responding to God's grace, and in that sense, they became an example and model to us all!

Why is systematic and proportional giving such an important aspect of the Christian life? Jesus answered that question for us when He said, "For where your treasure is, there your heart will be also" (Matt. 6:21). In other words, how we use our material possessions reflects our true relationship with God through Jesus Christ. This is why Scripture says more about this area of our lives than any other aspect of Christian living. And that's why it became a priority in Jacob's life once he became a true believer.

## A Reality Check

Does this mean a person is not a true Christian if he doesn't attend church regularly and tithe? Certainly not. But if we neglect personal and public worship on a consistent basis and neglect being generous with our time, talents, and treasures—especially when we know what God's will is for His children—we need to take a careful look at our relationship with God. Do we really know Him in a personal way? For example, if you've read this chapter, understand its message, and refuse to consider the principles we've just looked at without a sense of conviction and a desire to do God's will, perhaps you're not a true "son" or "daughter." Or perhaps you're simply living what Paul calls a worldly and carnal lifestyle as a Christian. But remember, if you're a true Christian, your heavenly Father will eventually discipline you for your disobedience. The author of the book of Hebrews made this very clear when he wrote, "Endure hardship as discipline; God is treating you as sons. For what son is not disciplined by his father? If you are not disciplined (and everyone undergoes discipline), then you are illegitimate children and not true sons" (Heb. 12:7–8).

## Personalizing These Principles

Use the following questions to evaluate your standing before God.

1. If you stood at the "door of heaven" and Jesus asked you why He should let you enter, what would you say? In the following list, check the answers you might give:

- ☐ I have been baptized.
- ☐ I'm a church member.
- ☐ I tithe.
- ☐ My good works outweigh my bad works.
- ☐ I go to confession.
- ☐ I attend religious services regularly.
- ☐ I pray every day.
- ☐ I'm a good parent.
- ☐ I don't steal.
- ☐ I live a good, moral life.

☐ I try to keep the Ten Commandments.

Do you realize that you may have checked all of the above and yet Jesus would turn you away? It's impossible to enter heaven by doing good works. This is why Paul wrote to the Ephesians: "For it is by grace you have been saved, through faith—and this not from yourselves, it is the gift of God—not by works, so that no one can boast" (Eph. 2:8–9).

There is only one answer that would be acceptable to Jesus Christ in allowing you to enter heaven. In essence, it's as follows:

> I put my faith in Jesus Christ for my salvation. I'm relying only on what He did for me when He died on the cross and rose again. I have confessed my sins and believe that the blood of Jesus Christ shed for me has washed those sins away. And because Jesus Christ rose from the dead, I too am alive and have eternal life. My faith is in the Lord Jesus Christ for my salvation—and in the Lord Jesus Christ alone.

2. What evidence is there in my life that I am a true believer?

☐ I worship God from my heart.

☐ I recognize His holiness.

☐ I use my talents to serve Jesus Christ and others.

☐ I use my time to carry out His purposes in the world.

☐ I give regularly and proportionately to both worship God and to help carry out His work.

☐ I am being transformed by the renewing of my mind.

☐ I am walking in the will of God.

☐ I am reflecting the fruit of the Spirit.

☐ Other: _____

## Set a Goal

As you evaluate your life in the light of Jacob's experience at Bethel, what goal do you need to set? Perhaps you have not been faithful in being generous with your material possessions. Whatever your need, write out a specific goal to make the change in your life that you feel you need to make to conform your life to God's will:

_____

_____

_____

_____

## Memorize the Following Scripture

*Jesus did many other miraculous signs in the presence of his disciples, which are not recorded in this book. But these are written that you may believe that Jesus is the Christ, the Son of God, and that by believing you may have life in his name.*

JOHN 20:30–31

## Growing Together

The following questions are designed for small-group discussion:

1. When did you come to know the Lord Jesus Christ as your personal Savior? Would you feel free to share with us when and how this happened?

2. Do you know you are a Christian but can't pinpoint the time or place? If you cannot, what is your basis for knowing for sure that you are a true believer?

3. If a person seems to be uncertain about his salvation, how would you help that person find assurance and a sense of security in Christ?

4. Do you know someone with whom you'd like to share the message of salvation? Would you tell us who it is so we can pray with you that you might have an opportunity to witness?

# Chapter 6

# Reaping What We Sow
### Read Genesis 29:1–28

$J$acob's personal encounter with God was real, and his new commit-ments were honest and sincere. The Lord's reassuring words gave him a new lease on life. His spirits were buoyed! The morning following his dream, he immediately continued on his journey (Gen. 29:1). When his response is translated literally, his new sense of motivation is obvious. "And Jacob *picked up his feet* and went to the land of the people in the east."

## *"Sweet to the Soul and Healing to the Bones"*

We've already noted that Jacob would have had to walk very rapidly from Beersheba to Bethel to cover fifty miles in one day. Evidently he even increased his speed for the next four hundred miles, not because he feared Esau, but because he was anxious to see God's purposes carried out in his life. It's quite amazing how good we can feel emotionally *and* physically when our spiritual house is in order. As one proverb states, "Pleasant words are a honeycomb, sweet to the *soul* and healing to the bones" (Prov. 16:24). Needless to say, God's words to Jacob were very "pleasant" when He told him He would be with him and care for him wherever he went (Gen. 28:15). God's promise certainly must have increased Jacob's energy—both psychologically and physically.

Jacob didn't realize, however, what lay ahead for him when he arrived in the vicinity of Haran. Ironically, he would see a replay of his own deceptive practices. This time, he would be the object of another man's

---

73

manipulation. He was going to reap what he had sown. But he really would not experience the full weight of this reality for another seven years!

## *Shepherds from Haran*

When Jacob arrived in the vicinity of Haran, he met a band of shepherds who were responsible for three flocks of sheep. They were friendly and cordial and answered Jacob's questions directly and openly. "My brothers," Jacob asked, "where are you from?" We can only imagine Jacob's emotional reactions when he discovered they were from Haran (29:4). His journey was almost over. If we had to walk from Dallas, Texas, to Kansas City, we would be able to identify with Jacob's excitement and relief!

But having arrived at his destination after a long and arduous trip was not the main source of Jacob's enthusiasm. The shepherds' answers to his next two questions brought an even more exciting response:

"Do you know Laban, Nahor's grandson?"

"Yes, we know him."

"Is he well?"

"Yes, he is, and *here comes his daughter Rachel with the sheep*" (29:5–6).

### A Nervous Moment

Jacob's communication with the shepherds must have become even more animated. "Look," he said, "the sun is still high; it is not time for the flocks to be gathered. Water the sheep and take them back to pasture" (29:7).

Was Jacob just being "Jacob"—telling a group of strangers how to handle their vocational responsibilities? Or was he simply nervous? Perhaps his emotions were running wild because of his new relationship with the God of Abraham and his father, Isaac? Was this simply "zeal without knowledge"?

We can only use our imagination to reconstruct what was going on in Jacob's mind and heart. We're not even certain how far away Rachel was when the shepherds identified her as Laban's daughter. But what we *do know* is that Jacob knew Laban was his mother's brother—a man he had never met. And he also knew that he was to find a wife from within his own family. He had to be wondering if Rachel was the girl he would eventually marry.[1]

## Déjà Vu

Personally, I think Jacob had a strong sense that this woman could be the wife God had chosen for him. He must have heard his own mother, Rebekah, share many times how she had come to the well near Haran—years ago now—and met Abraham's chief servant, Eliezer. He was there to find a wife for Jacob's father, Isaac, and his mother, Rebekah, of course, was the woman who appeared at the well.

We must remember that Jacob was a homebody—"a quiet man, staying among the tents" (25:27). He was very close to his mother emotionally, and it would have been natural for her to share this remarkable story with Jacob many times over the years. In fact, Rebekah may have reviewed her own dramatic story for her son before Isaac sent him off to Haran to find a wife among his relatives. In that sense, the remarkable way his mother met his own father would be very fresh in his mind. Rachel's sudden appearance then would certainly strike a familiar cord in his heart. It would be as if he were living out something he had heard many times before.

## A Need for Privacy

Whatever Jacob's thoughts at this moment, he wanted an opportunity to get acquainted with Rachel—alone—not with a group of shepherds looking over his shoulder and whispering among themselves about this unusual meeting between two cousins who had never met before. Consequently, he suggested—rather strongly—that they get on about their business, water their sheep, and move out to the open pasture. After all, there was a lot of time before sunset.

The shepherds, however, were not about to take orders from a stranger. "We can't," they replied, "until all the flocks are gathered and the stone has been rolled away from the mouth of the well. *Then* we will water the sheep" (29:8).

Various commentators have speculated regarding the shepherds' watering procedures. Why did they all wait for one another. After all, one man could remove the stone, although the text is clear that it was a "large" stone—probably difficult to move (29:2). I believe that their primary motive was social. After all, a shepherd's life was a lonely life much of the time, and meeting together to water their flocks gave all of them an opportunity to catch up on the latest gossip and visit with one another. But, for whatever reasons, the shepherds were not about to accommodate Jacob. This stranger wasn't going to dictate their schedule.

## An Adrenaline High

What happened next demonstrates Jacob's emotional state. He was so "pumped" psychologically that adrenaline must have been flooding his blood stream! First, when Rachel arrived on the scene, "he went over and rolled the stone away from the mouth of the well and watered his uncle's sheep" (29:10)—all by himself! As often happens in this kind of psychological state, human strength becomes almost superhuman.

As soon as he had completed this task, he "kissed Rachel and began to *weep aloud*" (29:11). At this point, his emotions boiled over and he was clearly out of control—which helps us to understand more fully why Jacob may have wanted the shepherds to leave. He knew he was inwardly about ready to explode!

Jacob's emotional intensity is understandable. Think for a moment about what he had experienced since he left Beersheba. He was on the run because his brother threatened to kill him. And "meeting God" in his dream at Bethel, Jacob came face-to-face with himself and his deceptive nature. Furthermore, he just met a beautiful woman he might one day marry. Embarrassing or not, Jacob let go of his emotions. He broke down and wept audibly and publicly—strangers or not!

### Rachel's Excitement

At this point, Jacob had already told Rachel that he was a "relative of her father and a son of Rebekah." Consequently, this "shepherd girl" was not afraid or shocked by his behavior. Since she had no doubt heard about the way her Aunt Rebekah had been whisked away by Eliezer many years before, she must have been intrigued with what was unfolding before her eyes. She was obviously excited and delighted as "she ran and told her father" (29:12). Jacob must have been full of nervous anticipation as he watched Rachel disappear over the nearest hill.

### What Will Her Daddy Think?

Fear of Laban's response must have gripped Jacob's heart. Imagine his relief when Laban responded so quickly. He wasted no time going to meet Jacob once he heard Rebekah's report. He, too, welcomed his nephew warmly. Imagine how Jacob felt when Rachel's father "embraced him and kissed him and brought him to his home." It was there that Jacob gave Laban all the details about what had happened. We simply read that he "told him all these things" (29:13).

## How Vulnerable Was Jacob?

I doubt that "all these things" included his family difficulties. Jacob was too shrewd to unload all his personal garbage. Rather, he probably picked up with his father's charge to find a wife among Rebekah's family. Perhaps the two of them compared notes about what had happened when Eliezer suddenly appeared years ago. Exchanging exact details of that unusual event would have been captivating and intriguing. Understandably, Laban responded, "You are my own flesh and blood" (29:14). Though he had never met Jacob before, there was too much common knowledge to believe otherwise.

## What about Jacob's Dream?

It's difficult to discern whether or not Jacob discussed his dream with Laban. If he did, there was no evidence that the divine significance of what happened impacted Laban. He had his own self-centered agenda, and as we'll see, his agenda certainly didn't reflect any specific concerns regarding God's divine will. His thoughts and actions were still driven by materialistic motivations—just as they were years before (24:29–31). Ironically, Laban was about to do to Jacob what Jacob had done to his father and to his brother.

## A Full Circle Experience

What happens next in this story illustrates the theme of this chapter. Jacob was going to reap what he had sown. Though he certainly had had a dramatic and soul-searching encounter with God at Bethel, he was still going to suffer the consequences of his sins.

## Subtle Manipulation

On the surface, it appears that Laban was magnanimous and generous in his relationship with Jacob. It was customary in his culture for a visitor to be entertained only three or four days without earning his stay, but Jacob had been in Laban's home a whole month, apparently without discussing any financial obligations. But Jacob had probably been working the whole time. After thirty days, Laban initiated a conversation by saying, "Just because you are a relative of mine, should you work for me for nothing? Tell me what your wages should be" (29:15).

Though Laban's suggestion sounds benevolent, he was definitely manipulating Jacob. The implication is clear; Laban didn't want to be obligated in any way to Jacob. Furthermore, he wanted to pay Jacob a salary that would probably be comparable to what he paid a household servant. Laban was definitely maneuvering himself into a position of control. C. F. Keil and F. Delitzsch capture Laban's intent when they state that his "selfishness comes out here under the appearance of justice and kindness."[2]

## Jacob Was Still "Jacob"

Before Laban raised the issue of wages, Jacob had been doing some thinking on his own. Though he had met God in a new way, he was still "Jacob." He was intelligent and cunning.

When he moved into Laban's home he quickly discovered that Laban had *two* daughters. Leah was the oldest and Rachel the younger. We can also assume that Jacob understood the custom that a father always gave his oldest daughter in marriage first. However, Jacob was not interested in Leah. She "had weak eyes, but Rachel was lovely in form, and beautiful" (29:17). From the day they met at the well, Jacob was attracted to Rachel, and his feelings of affection grew stronger during the month that followed. In fact, the Scriptures clearly state that "Jacob was in love with Rachel" (29:18).

## A Generous Offer

If Jacob understood the custom (which I believe he did) he faced a dilemma. How could he marry Rachel? She was the youngest. Jacob quickly discovered Laban's materialistic interests, and by appealing to Laban's selfishness, he apparently devised a plan to convince Laban to ignore the marriage custom. He was ready with an answer to Laban's question regarding wages. "I'll work for you seven years," Jacob responded, "in return for your *younger* daughter Rachel" (29:18).

Jacob knew that Laban wasn't about to come out on the losing end of this deal. This helps explain his generous offer and why he was willing to be so magnanimous with his time and energy. Though seven years is a long time to wait for the one you love, Jacob had clearly calculated the kind of "wages" that would entice Laban to look the other way when it came to social customs. Since Jacob loved Rachel so much, he was willing to make this personal sacrifice. In his mind, it would be well worth it!

Laban responded positively. Clearly, it was a good deal. After all, seven years of labor would calculate into an enormous sum of money. Hiding behind some very selfish motives, he said, "It's better that I give her to you than to some other man. Stay here with me" (29:19). But unknown to Jacob, Laban was no doubt already devising a plan to deceive him and to take advantage of his love for Rachel.

## Hard Work and Sincere Effort

Jacob enthusiastically went to work as he looked forward to his wedding day. Though he had not lost his ability to negotiate a good deal, at this point we see a man with a changed heart. Had he been the "old Jacob," he would have been plotting to circumvent this arrangement. For example, he could have played the role of matchmaker in order to find a husband for Leah, which would set Rachel free to marry him before he had fulfilled his seven-year commitment. However, there seems to be no thought of violating his agreement. We simply read that "Jacob served seven years to get Rachel, but they seemed like only a few days to him because of his love for her" (29:20).

Jacob kept careful and accurate records during this seven-year period. Can you imagine a tree with 2,555 notches (365 x 7)? We're not sure, of course, how Jacob calculated the time, but he did. When the seven years were up, he came to Laban and said, "Give me my wife. *My time is completed*, and I want to lie with her" (29:21).

## True Love

How many men today would be willing to do what Jacob did? This relationship involved more, much more, than infatuation and sexual attraction. Not once did the flame flicker as if to die out. The days and months and years flew by as Jacob anticipated his wedding day. This was true love!

Jacob's request to take Rachel as his wife tells us something else about Jacob. Not once had he violated Laban's or Rachel's trust by arranging a secret affair. Even in this Old Testament culture involving sexual freedom, Jacob had maintained moral purity. This, too, says something about Jacob's new heart and the purity of his love for Rachel.

## A Heartless Trick

On the surface, Laban agreed to fulfill his end of the bargain. He "brought together all the people of the place and gave a feast" (29:22). But Jacob was about to experience the surprise of his life! After the celebration, when it came time for Jacob and his bride to be alone, Laban substituted Leah for Rachel. In the darkness, Jacob didn't know the difference, and he culminated his marriage with Leah. In fact, he didn't realize what had happened until the next morning. Can you imagine the expression on his face when he opened his eyes and "there was Leah!" (29:25).

What irony! What satire! Today we'd say "the chickens had come home to roost!" In more theological terms, we might say, "Be sure your sins will find you out," or, more appropriately, *"We reap what we sow."*

What makes this even more ironic is that Laban probably knew nothing of Jacob's deceptive plot against his brother, Esau. Though Laban's behavior was cruel and heartless, God allowed it in Jacob's life to give him a visual picture of himself prior to his spiritual experience at Bethel. As we'll see, Jacob had a long way to go in becoming the man God wanted him to become. Even after seven years, his journey toward spiritual maturity was just beginning.

## What Goes Around, Comes Around

What had just happened to Jacob was indeed sad and painful. Initially, while Laban and his cohorts were probably "laughing up their sleeves," Jacob must have been boiling with anger. The embarrassment must have been almost more than he could bear. Imagine his frustration and anguish when he confronted Laban with three pointed questions:

"What is this you've done to me?"

"I served you for Rachel, didn't I?"

"Why have you *deceived* me?" (29:25)

Jacob's final question says it all! His own deception had come full circle. There are indeed some haunting correlations between what Jacob and his mother did to Isaac and Esau. In fact, the Hebrew word translated "beguiled" or "deceived" that Jacob used in confronting Laban is basically the same word his brother, Esau, used when he cried out in anguish and pain—"Isn't he rightly named *Jacob*? He has *deceived* me these two times: He took my birthright, and now he's taken my blessing!" (27:36).

Things happened so fast, Jacob probably didn't get the full impact of what transpired. But the full reality would gradually seep into his painful soul. He would understand emotionally how Esau must have felt that day when he came in from hunting and discovered that Jacob had deceived his father and taken away the blessing.

## A Masterpiece of Shameless Treachery

Laban's response to Jacob's interrogation was cruel and calculated: "It is not our custom here to give the younger daughter in marriage before the older one. Finish this daughter's bridal week; then we will give you the younger one also, in return for another seven years of work" (29:26–27).

When did Laban concoct this shameless scheme? I believe it happened seven years before, when Laban agreed to give Rachel to Jacob in turn for seven years of labor. This had been his thinking all along. He'd marry off his older daughter, Leah, and at virtually the same time (one week later) give Jacob Rachel. And knowing how much Jacob loved Rachel, Laban knew he could get another seven years of work!

This predetermined scheme raises some interesting questions. When did Leah become aware of this scam? What about Rachel? When did their mother discover what was in Laban's mind? Obviously, all three women would have to know at some point in time. Laban would have to calculate this carefully because Jacob would have discovered Laban's plan if Laban revealed it too quickly to his wife and daughters.

There's one clue in the text that the girl's mother had probably been a part of this scheme for some time. Laban used the plural pronoun "we" when he informed Jacob that "they" would give Rachel to him in one week—*if* he would work another seven years. Whatever the details, this *was* indeed a masterpiece of shameless treachery.

## Imagine Rachel's Plight

I believe Laban waited until the seven-year period was nearly over to reveal his nasty secret to Rachel. Rachel may have been tricked into silence—perhaps she was taken to an undisclosed place where she was supposedly waiting for her wedding night. However, you can imagine her state of mind and heart when she discovered what had happened! What if Jacob simply settled for Leah and headed back to Canaan? This question certainly had to be torturing her soul. And even if Jacob accepted her father's ultimate plan, how could she emotionally share her husband with her sister, Leah?

## Love Prevailed

Jacob's response probably surprised them all! Seeing he had no choice in the matter, and motivated by his deep love for Rachel, a love that would never die, he agreed to the plan and "worked for Laban another seven years" (29:30). When one week had gone by, Laban kept his word this time and gave Rachel to Jacob to be his second wife. Sadly, this was a terrible marital beginning for both Leah and Rachel. And it was horribly complicated by the fact that Jacob "loved Rachel more than Leah." This tragic event set the stage for problems that would fester and linger for years to come.

## Becoming God's Man Today

*Principles to Live By*

*Principle 1. When we violate the will of God in our lives, we always experience the natural consequences of our sins.*

"Do not be deceived," Paul wrote to the Galatians. "God cannot be mocked. A man reaps what he sows" (Gal. 6:7). This is a spiritual law that is just as predictable as a natural law. And it is what happened to Jacob. He sowed to please his sinful nature. And when that happens, Paul states that anyone who sows to please the flesh will from that very flesh "reap destruction" (6:8).

### Moral Consequences

The world today is filled with examples of what happens to people who ignore this spiritual law of reaping what you sow. Young people are being terribly deceived when they're told that sexual abstinence before marriage is an old-fashioned idea. The results of this sin pervade our culture. A multitude of babies are born out of wedlock. Young women, particularly, are often set adrift to bear the burden alone. Some choose abortion—another devastating result of following our sinful nature. Some marry under pressure and often do not understand what true love is all about. It's no wonder that these marriages often are doomed to failure—another result of sin.

## Lingering Guilt

Another negative result of violating the will of God is lingering guilt. As a pastor, I've seen this again and again in the lives of young women who have had abortions. Even though they attempted to convince themselves that what they were doing was a lawful and acceptable alternative to bringing a child into the world, they could not avoid the subsequent emotional trauma. In some instances, it led to denial, which in turn affected their marital relationships. The fact is that we cannot violate the will of God without suffering the consequences of our sins. Even believing it is not sinful will never eliminate God's spiritual laws and the results of violating those laws. We reap what we sow, and Jacob demonstrated this reality throughout his life.

*Principle 2. The degree to which we suffer the consequences of our sins depends on the nature of our sins.*

This principle is illustrated graphically in Paul's letter to the Romans. When men and women begin to turn away from God's eternal values, they naturally and unsuspectingly sink deeper into the mire of sin. The tentacles of evil subtly develop a strangle hold around their unsuspecting victims. Like the proverbial frog in the kettle, they gradually adjust to the new environment, and before they realize it, they are beyond "the point of no return."

Paul detailed this descent into the world that John described as "the cravings of sinful man, the lust of his eyes and the boasting of what he has and does" (1 John 2:16). He also described in detail the way men and women reap what they sow.

When we choose to deliberately violate the will of God, God eventually allows us to get trapped in our own sinful desires. Paul outlined this by describing three distinctive steps:

Step 1: "Therefore God gave them over in the sinful desires of their hearts to sexual impurity for the degrading of their bodies with one another" (Rom. 1:24). Here Paul described the result of heterosexual sin.

Step 2: "God gave them over to shameful lusts" (Rom. 1:26–27). Here Paul described the results of homosexual behavior.

Step 3: "He gave them over to a depraved mind, to do what ought not to be done" (1:28). Here Paul described "every kind of wickedness, evil, greed and depravity" (1:29).

Today, we're seeing this pattern displayed in our culture. Marriages are disintegrating. Sexual harassment and rape are at an all time high. The battle over abortion rages. More and more people are dying of AIDS, a disease closely related to homosexuality. The newspapers report senseless drug related murders daily. Sadly, the results of these sins affect people, not only in this life but eternally.

There is no question that the degree to which we suffer the consequences of our sins depends on the nature of our sins. We cannot avoid this reality.

*Principle 3. God sometimes allows us to suffer the consequences of our sins so that we might understand the pain we've caused in others' lives, and this understanding will create in us the desire to draw closer to God and treat others in a more Christlike manner.*

I believe this is one of the primary purposes the Lord had in mind when He allowed Jacob to experience what must have been almost identical emotions to those of his father, Isaac, and his brother, Esau. Furthermore, the Lord used some very similar circumstances, which would have certainly grabbed Jacob's attention. How could he miss the point that Leah was the older and Rebekah the younger—haunting memories of his own relationship with Esau. And how could he not remember his own deceptive antics when he suddenly realized that he had been deceived—when he awakened and "there was Leah!"

Frankly, I don't believe Jacob had any idea how his father and brother must have felt until he found himself in similar circumstances experiencing the same painful emotions. Suddenly—or gradually—it must have dawned on him what he had really done.

Today, there are also people who hurt others because of some sin in their lives. Eventually, they meet God personally, acknowledge their sins, accept forgiveness—and then go about rebuilding their own lives without giving a second thought to the people they've wounded.

## A Painful Experience

I'm reminded of a fellow pastor. We served together for many years and had a very trusting relationship. But then it happened: he became emotionally and sexually involved with a woman other than his wife. Through a series of providential circumstances his sin was discovered.

Both he and the woman confessed their sins publicly, but their subsequent behavior demonstrated that they hadn't truly repented and humbled themselves before God. In fact, they began to play the "martyr" role, generating sympathy. As often happens in this kind of situation, they eventually made themselves "victims" rather than taking the responsibility of being the ones who caused the problem. This was a terribly painful experience for me, since I had implicitly trusted both this man and woman, and I wanted to see both of them restored to fellowship with God and with their fellow believers.

A couple of years after their "fall from grace," the man came to my wife and me to seek forgiveness. We assured him we had already forgiven him—a long time ago—but with tears my wife shared the hurt she had seen in the lives of many, many people because of his sin. At that moment, he seemed to grasp more fully the reality of what he had done—not just to his wife—but to others. He, too, teared up as my wife shared the pain he had caused. I believe he reached a new level of understanding, although he still had a long way to go in terms of restoring his relationship with his own wife and his family.

In many respects, this illustrates what happened to Jacob. It took time for him to truly understand what he had done. Furthermore, it took a similar set of circumstances in his own life to bring him face-to-face with reality. God cannot use us as He would like when we are in a state of ignorance or denial. This is why He sometimes allows us to suffer the consequences of our sins. He wants us to understand the pain we've caused in others' lives so we can in turn draw closer to them and treat others in a more Christlike manner.

*Principle 4. No matter who or what caused the consequences of sin in our lives, God wants us to view pain and suffering as a means to be able to minister more effectively to others who are experiencing the same difficulties.*

Unfortunately, not all suffering is because of our own sins. For example, when children are abused by parents, they suffer the consequences of their parents' sins. When this abuse is sexual it is particularly devastating, often doing almost irreparable damage to a child's personality. In fact, I have several friends who were ritually abused in a satanic cult. With

God's help, they are trying desperately to rise above the results of their parents' sins in their lives. However, they struggle almost every day in ways that most of us never struggle. On the other hand, I see God using these people to minister to others in ways that most of us cannot.

## From Despair to Hope

The apostle Paul understood this principle. He not only suffered the results of his own sin when he was an unbeliever, but after he became a Christian he suffered for the cause of Christ. When he wrote his second letter to the Corinthians, he informed them that he and his fellow missionaries were "under great pressure." In fact, he wrote that this suffering was "far beyond" their "ability to endure," so that they "despaired even of life" (2 Cor. 1:8).

Paul, however, viewed this suffering as a means to enable him to minister to others. Thus he introduced this letter with these words: "Praise be to the God and Father our Lord Jesus Christ, the Father of compassion and the God of all comfort, who comforts us in all our troubles, so that we can comfort those in any trouble with the comfort we ourselves have received from God" (2 Cor. 1:3–4).

## Special Rewards

Though it is difficult to live with the results of someone else's sin, it is comforting to know you can understand another person's pain and minister to that individual in unique ways—ways others cannot. In fact, people often experience personal healing and relief from their own suffering by having the opportunity to focus on others' problems and help them to rise above their experiences and become productive members in the body of Christ. If you are a person who has innocently suffered, I believe you will be eternally rewarded in unique and abundant ways when you eventually stand at the Judgment Seat of Christ.

*Principle 5. No matter the cause of our pain and suffering and regardless of the results in our lives, God forgives the sins of the past. When God forgives us, He sees us as perfect in Christ.*

When we suffer the consequences of our sins or the sins of others in our lives, God is not punishing us for our sins. Rather—as stated above—we are simply suffering the natural consequences of sin. The reality is that God has forgiven us and His blood continues to cleanse us from all unrighteousness (1 John 1:9).

Again, the apostle Paul stands out as a supreme example. In his unsaved life, he was responsible for Stephen's death. Putting it bluntly, he was guilty of murder. However, he experienced God's forgiveness when he put his faith in Jesus Christ. Paul never forgot what he had done. But, he did not go through life focusing on his sin. Rather, he focused on God's grace and the forgiveness that he received through Christ.

He knew that if God could forgive him, He could forgive anyone. That was his message of hope to others. This is what he had in mind when he wrote to Timothy in his first letter: "Here is a trustworthy saying that deserves full acceptance: Christ Jesus came into the world to save sinners—of whom I am the worst. But for that very reason I was shown mercy so that in me, the worst of sinners, Christ Jesus might display his unlimited patience as an example for those who would believe on him and receive eternal life" (1 Tim. 1:15–16).

## Personalizing These Principles

Use the following questions to reflect on your life as Christian.

1. When I'm tempted to sin, do I stop and consider the natural consequences that will result if I walk out of God's will?

2. Do I understand that sin of any kind has a way of hardening my heart and leading me deeper into a way of life that brings even more serious consequences?

3. Do I understand that when I suffer the consequences of my sin that are similar to the hurt I've caused in others, it will help me get in touch with reality and stop blaming others for my self-created predicament? (In other words, this kind of experience breaks us out of the tendency to classify ourselves as "victims," when in reality, we've actually created the problem.)

4. Do I understand that the consequences of sin in my life—whether caused by others or myself—can help me minister more effectively to others who are experiencing the same consequences of sin as I am?

5. Have I experienced total forgiveness in Christ for what I've done that is out of God's will? Am I focusing on this forgiveness rather than on the consequences of my sin?

## Set a Goal

As you reflect on the principles in this chapter, select the one you need to practice more fully. For example, you may be focusing on the consequences of sin rather than on the forgiveness and freedom you can experience in Christ. Set a specific goal that will help you forget "what is behind" and to "press on toward the goal to win the prize" that God has called you to receive—namely, eternal rewards for being a faithful servant of Jesus Christ (Phil. 3:12–14).

_____

_____

_____

_____

## Memorize the Following Scripture

*Here is a trustworthy saying that deserves full acceptance: Christ Jesus came into the world to save sinners—of whom I am the worst. But for that very reason I was shown mercy so that in me, the worst of sinners, Christ Jesus might display his unlimited patience as an example for those who would believe on him and receive eternal life.*
1 Timothy 1:15–16

## Growing Together

The following questions are designed for small-group discussion:

1. Why is it that some people tend to suffer the consequences of sin more deeply, even when the sin seems to be identical to the sins of others?

2. We've all sinned (or been sinned against) and have suffered various consequences. Would you feel free to share how you've handled the consequences of sin in your life?

3. What can we do to be free from the consequences of sin and not allow the negative results to push us down and to keep us from being productive in our Christian lives?

4. How can we protect our children from repeating our mistakes?

5. In what way can we pray for you? Would you feel free to share an area of your life where the consequences of sin have kept you in bondage?

## Chapter 7

# A Modern-Day Opera

Read Genesis 29:30–30:1–24

Without even knowing what happened following Jacob's multiple marriages, anyone could easily predict some devastating results. You don't even have to be a marriage counselor to see the coming storm. What happened has all the earmarks of a modern day opera. Laban's deception set the stage for the worst kind of favoritism, jealously, competition, and lack of trust—all of which led to enormous unhappiness, tension, stress, anxiety, and anger. As the curtain falls on the final act, Rachel's sad and final words serve as an epitaph that characterized her married life.

## Two Pagan Practices

Though God had chosen Jacob's grandfather, Abraham, and his family out of a totally pagan culture that was permeated with all kinds of ungodly practices, pagan influences lingered for generations. There are two particular practices that created problems and pain for Jacob's family.

### Polygamy

Polygamy was not God's plan. If it had been, He would have created more than one wife for Adam. Polygamy was a result of sin entering the world, and wherever polygamy has been practiced, it has created unusual family problems. We'll see *why* as we look at what happened in Jacob's life.

It's true that God tolerated this practice in Israel, even among some of His chosen servants, such as David and Solomon. But it was not His perfect will and led to failure in these men's lives. It didn't even keep David from stealing another man's wife and committing adultery. It appears that the more women David had, the more he wanted. And in King David's case, it wasn't purely licentiousness and sexual passion; it involved power, pride, and ego.

### Surrogate Mothers

Another pagan practice that raised its ugly head in this story is when a man would father children through other women provided by their wives. This practice was actually written into the wedding contracts in the Babylonian culture. A wife who could not bear children was obligated to provide her husband with a woman who could. This practice, of course, is very strange to those of us living in a culture built on the moral laws of the Bible as embodied in the Ten Commandments given at Mount Sinai and raised to an even higher standard in the New Testament. But the facts are that Sarah, Abraham's wife, probably agreed to this practice when she married Abraham. This is why she offered Hagar, her maidservant, to Abraham when she was barren. She reverted to her pagan way of thinking (Gen. 16:1–2). All of this, of course, happened hundreds of years before God revealed the Law on Mount Sinai establishing specific moral directions for the children of Israel.

Laban, Abraham's nephew, never gave up this pagan practice. Otherwise he would not have tricked Jacob into marrying both Leah and Rachel. In fact, Laban still practiced idolatry. When Jacob eventually headed back to Canaan, Rachel actually stole some of his "household gods"—which also tells us something about Rachel's level of spirituality (31:30–32).

Against this cultural backdrop, let's look at the events and dynamics of this story. As we'll see, it's not a lovely, romantic story. But from God's perspective, it once again reveals His sovereign grace.

## *Setting the Stage*

In our last study, we speculated on what happened in the lives of Leah and Rachel prior to Laban's great deception. Leah probably cooperated out of mixed motives. She no doubt wanted to be married, but she certainly would not have relished the idea of entering a relationship under such difficult conditions. She must have been terribly embarrassed the morning after when Jacob opened his eyes and discovered she was not Rachel. How could she even maintain eye contact?

## Daddy Reigned Supreme!

Rachel, on the other hand, must have been fit to be tied! In no way would she have wanted to participate in this kind of scam. She loved Jacob and certainly wanted him for herself. But both girls were victims of a cultural system where daddy reigned supreme. In many respects, they had no choice. Their whole inheritance was at stake! To rebel against their father would be choosing a life of poverty—and perhaps prostitution—in order to survive. Laban had already demonstrated that he would be capable of threatening his daughters with these alternatives.

## The Predictable Happened

Once the marriages took place, the problems that already existed were amplified many times. Jacob was forced to live with a woman he didn't love. Leah was a constant reminder of Laban's heartless trick. There's no way Jacob would not be tempted to displace his anger toward Laban onto Leah. To complicate matters, every morning he awakened to face a new day of work, he would naturally think about the fact that in order to have Rachel as his wife, Laban had forced him into this seven-year obligation.

Leah also became the object of Rachel's resentment. If there was sibling rivalry before, you can imagine what happened once they were both married to the same man. Furthermore, research studies demonstrate that tensions are much greater in polygamous situations when a man has married sisters. It only complicates the predictable competition, jealousies, and resentments. What we're about to see confirms that conclusion.

Act I

### *Lust but Not Love*

Poor Leah was not loved by Jacob or Rachel. But God did not forsake her. He loved her still, as He does all people, no matter what our sins. God had mercy on her and "opened her womb," and she had *four sons in a row*—while Rachel remained barren. Obviously, Jacob's lack of love for Leah didn't keep him out of her tent! Whatever his motives—sympathy, gratification, duty—he did not reject Leah totally.

### Scene 1. Reuben: "He Has Seen My Misery"

When Leah's first son was born, we once again see her plight. She chose a name that reflected her emotional pain. Reuben literally means "See, a son"! However, the word also sounds like the Hebrew "He has seen my misery." Here are perhaps the saddest words Leah ever uttered: "Surely my husband will love me now" (29:32). Unfortunately, her hopes were dashed but not her ability to get pregnant.

### Scene 2. Simeon: "One Who Knows"

Leah conceived again, and when she gave birth, she said, "Because the Lord heard that I am not loved, he gave me this one too" (29:33). She named her second son Simeon, which means "one who knows."

One of the redeeming features that grew out of Leah's pain is that it evidently drove her to prayer. She probably spent hours pouring out her heart to God, just as Hannah did many years later when she wept and prayed "in bitterness of soul" (1 Sam. 1:10).

Obviously, Leah could not share her deep feelings of anxiety with Jacob. He would not understand. Nor would he *want* to understand. But she did share her frustration with God. He became her Source of strength and she acknowledged her gratitude to the Lord with the very name she gave her son.

### Scene 3. Levi: "Attached"

Leah named her third son Levi, a word that in Hebrew means something like the English word "attached." She affirmed this definition with her own exclamation when her son was born: "Now at last my husband will become *attached* to me, because I have borne him three sons" (Gen. 29:34). In other words, how could he not love her since she had given him three boys in a row and Rachel had born him none?

What a pathetic picture! Jacob continued to love Rachel and to reject Leah. There was no emotional bonding whatsoever. Though sexually intimate, there was no emotional and spiritual relationship. But Leah was still hoping against hope that her ability to continue to bear children would win Jacob's love. Alas, it didn't happen!

### Scene 4. Judah: "Praise"

When Leah gave birth to her fourth son, she had come to the conclusion that she might as well give up on winning Jacob's love and attention. Understandably, she didn't want to set herself up for another disappointing experience. Consequently, she turned her thoughts heavenward and said, "This time I will praise the Lord" (29:35). She named her fourth son Judah, which sounds like the Hebrew word for *praise*.

Act II

## *Jacob's "Catch-22"*

At some time when Leah was bearing children, Rachel's jealousy reached a point of despair. Her anger inevitably led to intense depression. She had Jacob's love, but she couldn't conceive. In agony and bitterness she cried out to Jacob, "Give me children, or I'll die!" (30:2).

Rachel's verbal explosion threatened Jacob. It was an accusatory statement; she was blaming him for her barrenness. Predictably, Jacob responded with his own anger: "Am I in the place of God, who has kept you from having children?" (30:2). Jacob was terribly irritated. This was something over which he had no control. It was particularly frustrating since he had been spending a great majority of his time with Rachel. What else could he do? He found himself in a no-win situation.

## Scene 1. Dan: "He Has Vindicated"

Rachel must have reached an extremely low point in her life to do what she did next. Though it was culturally acceptable—and even an obligation if her husband insisted—Rachel must have been at her wits' end to give her servant girl, Bilhah, to Jacob. Jacob hadn't requested this arrangement since Leah had already borne him four sons. But to please Rachel, he cooperated.

Bilhah bore Jacob two sons. In both instances, Rachel's response is very telling. She named the first boy Dan, which means "he has vindicated." Elaborating on her reason for this name, she said, "God has vindicated me; he has listened to my plea and given me a son" (30:6).

## Scene 2. Naphtali: "My Struggle"

When Bilhah gave birth to her second son, Rachel named him Naphtali, which in Hebrew means "my struggle." She revealed her heart and her motives when she cried out with glee, "I have had a great struggle with my sister, and I have won" (30:8). How sad! Her "victory" was hollow and pathetic.

The picture is clear. From the moment Leah and Rachel had married Jacob—and even before—they had been in a power struggle. They were vying for Jacob's attention. From the birth of her very first son, Leah was determined to win Jacob's affection, and with the birth of each child, Rachel became more and more frustrated and angry. Ironically, she had Jacob's love, but she couldn't bear a child—a state of affairs that was considered disgraceful and very disappointing in her culture.

## Act III

### *Fighting Fire with Fire*

While all of this was happening, Leah's emotions were not in neutral. Though she had resigned herself temporarily to a "loveless" marriage, she also became jealous when Rachel's maid gave her children. Since she could no longer get pregnant (29:35), she fought fire with fire.

## Scene 1. Gad: "Good Fortune"

Leah insisted that Jacob continue to give her children through her maidservant, Zilpah. Again, Jacob cooperated. The first son was named Gad, which in Hebrew means "good fortune." Elaborating on her happiness, she said, "What good fortune!" (30:11). Literally, she was saying "a troop is coming!" In other words, in her mind this was just the beginning. I'm sure she wanted her response to get back to Rachel. In her mind, the race was on!

## Scene 2. Asher: "Happy"

Zilpah bore a second son, and this time Leah named him Asher, which means "happy." Again elaborating on her good fortune, she said, "How happy I am! The women will call me happy" (30:13).

The battle between Leah and Rachel was raging. Imagine what Jacob was thinking and feeling! At times, he may have been amused, but he must have often thought about Laban and what he had done to get him into this mess. On the other hand, it's possible he realized more and more that the real cause of his problems were his own sinful actions that began years before in his relationship with Esau. Seeing two sisters battle it out at close range for positions of prestige and to gain attention must have served as a mirror of his own battle with Esau.

## Act IV

### *Leah Wins Again*

## Scene 1. The Mandrake Plants

The next maneuver by Leah demonstrates the extent to which some people will go to please themselves and hurt others. Her son,

Reuben, found some mandrake plants out in the field and brought them to his mother. Leah had no doubt shared her frustration with her eldest son, and wanting to help, he presented her with what these people believed to be an aphrodisiac that would help a woman get pregnant. Clearly, he wanted his mother to be happy and to continue to win the battle over Rachel. How sad when children get involved in parental conflict.

Leah had an edge in this raging battle. The family grapevine—probably by design—got the "mandrake message" back to Rachel. Chagrined and still feeling sorry for herself, she came out of her tent begging Leah to share the plants with her. But Leah was ready with a very pointed and revealing retort: "Wasn't it enough that you took away my husband? Will you take my son's mandrakes too?" (30:15). With this response she was openly sharing what she had felt all along from the very first moment Jacob married Rachel. Leah had been on the outside looking in. In her heart she did not really feel that Jacob was her husband in the true sense of the word. The reason, as we've seen, is obvious: Jacob didn't love Leah.

But at this point, Rachel's back was against the wall. She appears beaten down. "Very well," she said, "he can sleep with you tonight in return for your son's mandrakes" (30:15). A very revealing statement. Though Leah had an edge in this emotional war, Rachel was still in control of the relationship. Jacob was not spending time with Leah. He was not about to visit Leah's tent without Rachel's permission. This was probably the way that he had decided to resolve the conflict and why Leah accused Rachel of "taking away her husband."

Whether or not Leah had expected this response, she wasted no time in taking action. That very evening she met Jacob as he came home from work. In fact, she "went out to meet him" *before* he even arrived on the scene. She did not *ask* him to be with her that night; she *told* him! "You *must* sleep with me," she said. "I have hired you with my son's mandrakes" (30:16).

How many times had Leah begged Jacob to spend the night with her? And how many times had Jacob said no, realizing that he would have to deal with Rachel's feelings? But at this point, Leah knew that he would have no excuse. Rachel had given her permission. Knowing this, Jacob cooperated (30:16).

## Scene 2. A Plan That Backfired!

Rachel was in for an incredible shock: Leah got pregnant—not once, but *three more times*. She gave birth to two more sons plus a daughter. The first boy she named Issachar, which sounds like the Hebrew word for "reward." She named the second boy Zebulun, which probably means "honor." And she named her daughter Dinah. Evidently, Jacob decided to continue to visit Leah's tent, no matter how Rachel felt about it! Even though he loved Rachel, he may have been retaliating because of her constant resentment and bickering—and making him the scapegoat.

Predictably, Leah was elated. When Issachar was born, she said, "God has rewarded me for giving my maidservant to my husband" (30:18). When Zebulun arrived on the scene, she said, "God has presented me with a precious gift" (30:20). However, her concluding remarks are a reflection of her continuing struggle to be accepted by Jacob. "*This time* my husband will treat me with honor, because I have borne him six sons" (30:20).

How sad! She has spent all of these years trying to win her husband's approval, but it never happened. Leah spent the rest of her life in a loveless marriage, even though she had borne half of the sons who would be the fathers of half the tribes of Israel.

### Act V

## *Rachel's Reprieve*

In all of this God did not forget Rachel. She had suffered long enough. Though He had rewarded Leah with sons because of the way she had been treated, He eventually allowed Rachel to become pregnant. The text reads, "Then God remembered Rachel; he *listened to her* and opened her womb" (30:22).

This raises some interesting questions. When did Rachel actually pray about her predicament? When did she specifically ask God to give her children? Is it possible that during this whole time, she had tried to control the situation and work it out on a purely human level, pleading with Jacob rather than with God?

Ironically, she probably learned an important lesson from Leah. There's no question she would have gotten the message loud and clear through the family grapevine that Leah had consulted God about her own frustration.

## Scene 1. Joseph: "May He Add"

Whatever prompted Rachel to pray, God responded. We read that "she became pregnant and gave birth to a son and said, "God has taken away my disgrace" (30:23). She named him Joseph, which actually means "may he add." Rachel herself gives us an interpretation of what she had in mind. The name Joseph was actually the essence of another specific prayer. Elaborating, she said, "May the Lord add to me another son" (30:24b).

## Scene 2. Benjamin: "Son of My Right Hand"

God answered Rachel's prayer for another son, but it would happen later, sometime after Jacob had fulfilled his seven-year commitment. In fact, they were on their way back to Jacob's original homeland.

Ironically, Rachel died in childbirth. It was after Jacob had returned to Bethel, the place where he had encountered God years before. We read: "Then they moved on from Bethel. While they were still some distance from Ephrath, Rachel began to give birth and had great difficulty. And as she was having great difficulty in childbirth, the midwife said to her, 'Don't be afraid, for you have another son.' As she breathed her last—for she was dying—she named her son Ben-Oni. But his father named him Benjamin" (35:16–18).

The name Rachel gave her second son literally means "son of my trouble." She knew she was dying and she wanted her son's name to reflect her predicament and perhaps her whole married life.

Jacob disagreed! He changed the boy's name to Benjamin, which means "son of my right hand." Perhaps Jacob's pride was involved in this decision. However, it's my opinion that Jacob did not want to remember Rachel in this way. She was his first love ever since they married, and at her death, he wanted everyone to know it!

At this point, the curtain falls on what could be called a modern-day opera—a tragic story laced with sadness, joy, competition, jealousy, and finally death. In the last moments of this incredible final scene, "Rachel died and was buried on the way to Ephrath (that is, Bethlehem)" (35:19).

How ironic that all this was in God's overall sovereign plan. Ephrath (Bethlehem) was the very place that Jesus Christ the promised Seed of Abraham would be born.

## Becoming God's Man Today

*Principles to Live By*

There are some obvious lessons in this story. Even though this was a polygamous marriage including other pagan practices—such as providing children through surrogate mothers—what happened still speaks to us today.

*Principle 1. Polygamy or being involved sexually with more than one man or woman in our lives in any form other than marriage is not God's perfect will.*

God intended that a man have one woman in his life and one woman only—his wife. Conversely, God intended that a woman have only one man in her life—her husband. This is the plan God established in the beginning before sin entered the world.

This is also why Paul stated that one of the most important requirements for a man who is a spiritual leader (an elder, a pastor, or a deacon) is that he be the "husband of but one wife" (1 Tim. 3:2,12; Titus 1:6). In other words, God wants a spiritual leader to be morally pure. He has a very high moral standard for *all* of His children but especially for those who are leading others.

God's perfect will is that a marriage relationship be permanent. Jesus made this very clear when He responded to the Pharisees' question about divorce. He quoted Moses and then gave His own addendum: "'Haven't you read,'" he replied, "'that at the beginning the Creator made them male and female,' and said, 'For this reason a man will leave his father and mother and be united to his wife, and the two will become one flesh'? So they are no longer two, but one. Therefore, what God has joined together let man not separate" (Matt. 19:4–6).

Jesus went on to explain that the law of Moses allowed for divorce because of sin, and when persistent marital unfaithfulness takes place, divorce is an option—even today (19:7–9). But again, Jesus emphasized that this is not God's ideal plan.

The implication is clear. When we violate God's perfect will in this matter, we will suffer the consequences—and so will our children. Again, it is the spiritual law of reaping and sowing we looked at in the previous chapter. We've seen this graphically illustrated in Jacob's life when he got involved in a polygamous relationship. Though the cultural arrangement was different, the dynamics were similar to any marital relationship that involves more than one woman or more than one man.

Today we see the same emotional results: jealousy, competition, anger, rejection, insensitivity, grief, confusion, and sadness. As we'll see in future installments of this ongoing saga, the most devastating results take place in our children when we violate God's will in these matters. Unfortunately, I could give hundreds of contemporary illustrations.

*Principle 2. God can create something beautiful out of something that is ugly, sinful, and sad.*

God did this in specific ways even in this tragic story. Woven throughout are rays of sunshine that break through the clouds that enveloped this Old Testament family. Leah experienced answers to prayer even though she lived her life in a loveless marriage. Rachel eventually bore two sons that brought her joy in the midst of her feelings of disgrace.

But more importantly, this story demonstrates that God uses weak and sinful human beings and through them and in spite of them accomplishes His purposes in the world.

## God Used What He Had

Think for a moment what happened. These twelve men—all sons of Jacob, but sons of four different women—formed the basis of the twelve tribes of Israel. In spite of the weaknesses and sins of their parents, and the sins of these twelve men, God sovereignly chose them and fulfilled His promises to Abraham that he would produce "a great nation" (Gen. 12:2). God worked with what He had. The facts are, anywhere God looked on planet Earth, there were no human beings that were righteous or living in His will (Rom. 3:10–18).

But we must look beyond God's initial redemptive step to see His ultimate goal—to bring a Savior into the world who would bring into being a wonderful, new, and dynamic entity: the Church. Paul described this as a wonderful "mystery" that was revealed in God's providential timing (Eph. 3:4). It includes both Jews and Gentiles. We are "members together of one body, and sharers together in the promise in Christ Jesus" (3:6).

## The Mystery Revealed

When Jesus Christ came to planet Earth, the world was in a dismal mess. Though there were some in Israel who were attempting to keep the law, the great majority were still living like Jacob. And those who were attempting to be righteous could not keep the law perfectly, thus becoming aware that they needed a savior. That too was in God's plan. As Paul stated in his letter to the Galatians, "So the law was put in charge to lead us to Christ that we might be justified by faith" (Gal. 3:24).

When Jesus came, the Gentile world was woefully trapped in the mire of sin, even more than the Jews. Though there were some Gentiles, like Cornelius, who were positively influenced by God-fearing Jews (Acts 10:1–48), the great majority had become futile in their thinking. As Paul stated to the Ephesians, "They are darkened in their understanding and separated from the life of God because of the ignorance that is in them due to the hardening of their hearts" (Eph. 4:18).

## We All Need a Savior

In the fullness of time, Jesus Christ came into the world to create something brand new out of sinful humanity. He revealed His grace in Jesus Christ, redeemed all who receive Him as Lord and Savior, and sent His Holy Spirit to indwell His newborn children and to guarantee their eternal inheritance (Eph. 1:13–14).

Since the first century, God has been working out the plan He designed "before the creation of the world," that we might become "holy and blameless in his sight" (Eph. 1:4). Just as God worked with what He had in the Old Testament era, He has worked with what He had available in the New Testament era, and even today. In many respects, we are no different than Jacob or Leah or Rachel—or even Laban. We all need a Savior, and without His spiritual guidance we are doomed to failure—now and eternally. With Paul we must cry out, "The sting of death is sin, and the power of sin is the law. But thanks be to God! He gives us the victory through our Lord Jesus Christ" (1 Cor. 15:56).

### Personalizing These Principles

Use the following questions to reflect on your own life as a Christian.

1. To what extent do I take God's moral codes seriously—in my own life, in the lives of my children, and in culture generally?

2. What specific steps have I taken to guard my spiritual and moral life?

3. If I have failed God morally, have I sought God's forgiveness? Have I accepted that forgiveness, or am I subtly attempting to atone for my sins by punishing myself?

## Set a Goal

As you reflect on the principles in this chapter, what do you need to do to guard your moral life? Set a specific goal:

_____

_____

_____

_____

## Memorize the Following Scripture

*You were taught, with regard to your former way of life, to put off your old self, which is being corrupted by its deceitful desires; to be made new in the attitude of your minds; and to put on the new self, created to be like God in true righteousness and holiness.*
EPHESIANS 4:22–24

## Growing Together

The following questions are designed for small-group discussion:

1. What causes the greatest temptation today for the average Christian man?

2. What specific steps have you taken to guard your moral and spiritual life?

3. How important is it to have open communication with our wives in the area of sexual temptations? Would you share how you accomplish this goal?

4. How can we keep communication open with our wives in a sensitive, nonthreatening way?

5. What specific needs do each of us have that we can pray about?

# Chapter 8

## *Change Points*
### Read Genesis 30:25–31:13

*A*ll of us experience "change points" in our lives—events, situations, or crises that forever alter the way we think and act. This was certainly true of Jacob.

## *Change Points in Jacob's Life*

The first major change point involved his collusion with his mother to deceive his father, Isaac, and his brother, Esau. As a result, he had to run for his life (Gen. 27:41; 28:10).

The second change point was his encounter with God at Bethel, where he built an altar to the Lord and vowed to serve God as the one true God. More specifically, he promised God that he would give back to the Lord a tenth of all that God gave him (28:20–22). This was a true conversion experience.

The third change point involved his uncle's deception. After Laban had promised to give Rachel to Jacob to be his wife in exchange for seven years of work, Laban slipped his eldest daughter, Leah, into Jacob's tent on his wedding night. Though Laban did make good on his promise one week later, Jacob now had two wives—one of them he didn't choose or love. This was probably one of the most traumatic change points in terms of ongoing emotional pain, not only for Jacob but for his whole family. He could not turn and run as he had done when he deceived his father. Rather, he had to make the best of a polygamous situation.

In this chapter, we will see that Jacob experiences another revolutionary change point, one destined to eventually bring him full circle and back home to make peace with his immediate family. However, the change was not abrupt or instantaneous. But I'm getting ahead of the story!

## A Dramatic Dialogue

### Jacob's First Recitation

> After Rachel gave birth to Joseph, Jacob said to Laban, "Send me on my way so I can go back to my own homeland. Give me my wives and children, for whom I have served you, and I will be on my way. You know how much work I've done for you." (Gen. 30:25–26)

This change point in Jacob's life was associated with Joseph's birth, Rachel's first born. Thus we read, "*After* Rachel gave birth to Joseph, Jacob said to Laban" (30:25a).

God had mercy on Rachel and opened her womb (30:22). Perhaps for the first time in seven years, Jacob experienced a degree of peace that he had not known before in his relationship with the woman he truly loved. One can only imagine the hundreds of times he had seen Rachel cry herself to sleep after encountering her incredible mood swings. Though her childless plight was not his fault, he was often the scapegoat!

Whatever the psychological dynamics, Jacob decided it was time to make a change—to seek his father-in-law's permission to return to his own homeland. Consequently, he pumped up his courage and approached Laban, asking to be released from his authority. Jacob could not simply pack his bags and leave. The authority structure in this Eastern extended family was far more complex and restrictive—as it is even today some places in the Eastern culture. There was a shared ownership even of his wives and children, which is clear from the text when he said, "Give me my wives and children, for whom I have served you" (30:26). To leave without Laban's permission and blessing could lead to outright war within the family clan.

### Laban's First Response

> But Laban said to him, "If I have found favor in your eyes, please stay. I have learned by divination that the Lord has blessed me because of you." He added, "Name your wages, and I will pay them." (Gen. 30:27–28)

On the surface, Laban's reaction to Jacob's request was pleasant and cordial. After all, he knew how much he had deceived and angered Jacob who had faithfully served him. But more importantly, Laban's obsequious response was motivated by his own selfish desires. Like most of what Laban did, down deep he was thinking of himself. He was smart enough to realize that much of his wealth resulted from his association with Jacob. In fact, he let Jacob know it was while engaging in some kind of religious activity ("divination") that he learned that God had blessed him because of Jacob. Whether or not Laban was telling the truth is debatable. On the other hand, he may have gotten involved in some kind of witchcraft. Nevertheless, knowing what we know about Laban's behavior in the past raises serious questions regarding his integrity. Understandably, Jacob didn't trust his uncle—which is reflected in his response to Laban's suggestion to "name his wages."

## Jacob's Second Recitation

Jacob said to him, "You know how I have worked for you and how your livestock has fared under my care. The little you had before I came has increased greatly, and the Lord has blessed you wherever I have been. But now, when may I do something for my own household?" (Gen. 30:29–30)

Jacob responded to Laban's invitation to "name his wages" with caution—and wisdom. He let Laban know rather candidly that it didn't call for an act of "divination" to discover why he had experienced material prosperity. Rather, it was very obvious that it was a combination of factors—especially Jacob's faithfulness and hard work (30:29). At this point in the dialogue, Jacob appealed to whatever sense of integrity and fairness might be present in Laban's heart. "But now," Jacob inquired, "when may I do something for my own household?" (30:30).

## Laban's Second Response

"What shall I give you?" he asked. (Gen. 30:31a)

It's obvious Jacob had thought carefully about *what* to say and *how* to say it—going over the possible responses and counterresponses again and again in his mind. Jacob was clearly in control of this conversation, and it was heading exactly where he wanted it to go!

## Jacob's Third Recitation

"Don't give me anything," Jacob replied. "But if you will do this one thing for me, I will go on tending your flocks and watching over them: Let me go through all your flocks today and remove from them every speckled or spotted sheep, every dark-colored lamb and every spotted or speckled goat. They will be my wages. And my honesty will testify for me in the future, whenever you check on the wages you have paid me. Any goat in my possession that is not speckled or spotted, or any lamb that is not dark-colored, will be considered stolen." (Gen. 30:31b–33)

Jacob's lack of trust in Laban is now clearly obvious in his third response. He knew he had to come up with a protective plan, one that would shield him from Laban's consistent tendency to be dishonest and manipulative. After all, if Laban had deceived him as he had done with Leah and Rachel, he certainly could not be trusted in an employment relationship. Consequently, Jacob refused to accept a cash settlement or a regular salary. Rather, he proposed a "commission structure" that was so weighted in Laban's favor that he couldn't refuse the offer. Furthermore, it was a plan whereby Laban could monitor Jacob's activities. There seemed to be no way Jacob could be dishonest with this arrangement. Laban could check up on him regularly, which Jacob made very clear to Laban when he said, "And my honesty will testify for me in the future, whenever you check on the wages you have paid me" (30:33).

## Laban's Third Response

"Agreed," said Laban. "Let it be as you have said." That same day he removed all the male goats that were streaked or spotted, and all the speckled or spotted female goats (all that had white on them) and all the dark-colored lambs, and he placed them in the care of his sons. Then he put a three-day journey between himself and Jacob, while Jacob continued to tend the rest of Laban's flocks. (Gen. 30:34–36)

When it came to recognizing a good deal, Laban was no dummy. In fact, he specialized in taking advantage of others. He immediately agreed to Jacob's proposal. But notice he did so with an apparent sense of distrust. It was such a good deal that Laban took no chances on some kind of hidden agenda. Consequently, he took control of the situation. It was *he* who "removed all the male goats that were streaked or spotted, and all the speckled or spotted female goats . . . and all the dark-colored lambs." It was *he* who placed them "in the care of *his sons*." Furthermore, it was *he* who "put a three-day journey between himself and Jacob, while Jacob continued to tend the rest of Laban's flocks." Clearly, Laban didn't trust Jacob, which was no doubt a projection of his own inner motives.

I'm reminded of an experience that my brother-in-law shared with me several years ago regarding his own business. For a number of years he owned a car dealership. One day a man came in to purchase an automobile. Eventually, my brother-in-law made a proposal, allowing a certain amount on the customer's old car with a cash settlement on the new one. All during the process it was very discernible that the customer didn't trust my brother-in-law, not only from what he said, but from his body language. Everything he said and did revealed that he "intuitively" knew my brother-in-law had a hidden agenda. Eventually, however, they agreed on a deal.

In a day or so, the customer came back to pick up the new car. He left his old car on the lot and drove away in the new one. Not bothering to look at the trade-in, my brother-in-law asked one of his employees to park it in the back lot.

Several weeks later, another customer came in to buy a used car. My brother-in-law immediately thought of that trade-in. To his amazement, when he took the new customer to look at the car, he discovered the previous skeptical owner had removed all the original tires—which were almost brand new—and had replaced them with bald ones. In fact, he had even replaced the back tires with different rims that weren't original to the car.

The point is this. Laban didn't trust Jacob because of his own deceitful heart. He was projecting his own dishonest motives on his son-in-law, just as the customer was projecting his own dishonesty on my brother-in-law. Dishonest and manipulative people often distrust others because of their own hidden and sinful agendas.

## A Mysterious Strategy

Ironically, Jacob *did* have a hidden agenda! In that sense, Laban's cautions are not without some justification. However, as we'll see, Jacob's strategy was rooted in an unusual experience.

### Superstitious Breeding

Jacob clearly outsmarted Laban on this deal. By rights, not one of Laban's sheep or goats should have borne spotted or striped animals.

After all, Jacob's flocks were three days removed—about fifteen miles away. There was no way for Jacob's animals to breed with Laban's, which was part of Laban's reason for establishing this distance.

However, Jacob had a plan, partly based on superstition and partly based on reality. He "took fresh-cut branches from poplar, almond and plane trees and made white stripes on them by peeling the bark and exposing the white inner wood of the branches." His next step was to place "the peeled branches in all the watering troughs, so that they would be directly in front of the flocks when they came to drink." Then, an unusual thing happened. We read that "when the flocks were in heat and came to drink, they mated in front of the branches. And, lo and behold, "they bore young that were streaked or speckled or spotted." As a result, Jacob multiplied the spotted and streaked animals for himself—which was part of the agreement he had with Laban (30:37–40).

## Selective Breeding

Jacob did one other thing that outfoxed Laban. Along with the "peeled branches" approach, he selectively bred only strong animals. Consequently, Jacob's flocks eventually became robust and very productive. As a result, we read that Jacob "grew exceedingly prosperous and came to own large flocks, and maidservants and menservants, and camels and donkeys" (30:43).

This is indeed a strange development. I grew up on a farm and learned how to breed animals. Though selective breeding is certainly a scientific approach for developing a strain of animals characterized by excellence, there is no way to scientifically explain the "branch method" Jacob used to cause these solid colored animals to produce striped and spotted offspring. What we read is based upon pure superstition. But, it still happened!

## *A Reflective Explanation*

What happened? How do we explain all of this? Frankly, I wrestled with these questions for some time. Then as I discovered, as usually happens, the answer is found in the Scriptures themselves.

## Increased Hostility

The predictable happened when Jacob's flock increased. Laban's attitude toward Jacob changed dramatically. In fact, Laban frequently changed his agreement with Jacob. When reporting this to Rachel and Leah, Jacob said, "Your father has cheated me by changing my wages ten times. However, he continued, "God has not allowed him to harm me" (31:7).

This indicates the intense jealousy and anger Laban felt toward Jacob. It also reveals his deceitful and dishonest heart. Laban never was sincere when he made the agreement in the first place.

Ironically, every time Laban changed the arrangement, the plan backfired. When he told Jacob the speckled animals would be his wages, the flocks gave birth to speckled young. When Laban said that streaked animals would be his wages, the flocks bore streaked young (31:8).

## Spiritual Insight

As Jacob reflected upon the whole process, he clearly recognized that God had caused all this to happen. This is apparent in his report to Rachel and Leah. Notice the following statements:

➤ "The God of my father has been with me" (31:5b).

➤ "God has not allowed him [Laban] to harm me" (31:7b).

➤ "God has taken away your father's livestock and has given them to me" (31:9).

## A Revealing Dream

At this point, Jacob reveals what he knew before he ever made the initial deal with Laban. He had a dream, a dream that must have taken place before Jacob had his discussion with Laban. Perhaps it happened during or after Rachel's pregnancy with Joseph when Jacob asked Laban to allow him to return to his homeland (30:25). Jacob's reflection speaks for itself: "In breeding season I once had a dream in which I looked up and saw that the male goats mating with the flock were streaked, speckled or spotted. The angel of God said to me in the dream, 'Jacob.' I answered, 'Here I am.' And he said, 'Look up and see that all the male goats mating with the flock are streaked, speckled or spotted, for I have seen all that Laban has been doing to you. I am the God of Bethel, where you anointed a pillar and where you made a vow to me. Now leave this land at once and go back to your native land'" (31:10–13).

With this perspective, we can understand more fully and even very specifically what motivated Jacob to approach Laban and to seek his permission to return to his "own homeland" (30:25).

*First,* on an occasion when Jacob was breeding his animals, God appeared to him and revealed the "streaked, speckled or spotted" idea.

*Second,* God told Jacob he was not unaware of Jacob's ill treatment—implying that He was going to do something about it (31:12b).

*Third,* God reminded Jacob of his new commitment and vow that he had made when He appeared to him in a dream at Bethel; namely, the altar he built and the vow he made to give a tenth of all he had if God provided (31:13a).

*Fourth,* God told Jacob very directly in his dream that he should leave the land at once and return to his "native land" (31:13b).

The content of this dream evidently launched Jacob into his discussion with Laban. However, something seemingly happened. Rather than trusting God to enable him to leave immediately or "at once"—as God had told him to—Jacob reverted to his old ways, attempting to figure out a way to outsmart Laban and make things happen. Thus, what appears to be "magic" was a miracle of God that would have happened regardless of Jacob's superstitious methods. It was the Lord who increased Jacob's flocks, in spite of his efforts to manipulate the situation.

Note, however, that Jacob suffered some difficult consequences because he didn't consult God and discover *His* methods for leaving immediately. Laban's sons turned against Jacob (31:1). In turn, Laban became angry and changed his wages ten times (31:7a). Evidently, things became so tense that Jacob feared for his life (31:7b). However, in spite of Jacob's reversion to his old ways, God remembered Jacob's Bethel commitments and knew he meant what he had said. God also remembered His promises to Abraham to build a great nation from his offspring in order to eventually bring the Messiah into the world to be a blessing to all humankind (Gen. 12:1–3). This dramatic story once again reveals God's sovereignty in carrying out His redemptive plan in the world.

## Becoming God's Man Today

*Principles to Live By*

**Principle 1. We must be on guard against reverting to our pagan and/or human ways of doing things even when we're attempting to do God's will.**

Please don't misunderstand. God generally does not give us "divine methods" to carry out His plans and purposes in this world. Yet, He outlines very clearly *what* He wants us *to do*, allowing us freedom to select methods that will enable us to carry out His will most effectively. However, our methods should always be in harmony with God's divine plan. Putting it another way, we should not work against God's will by using means that restrict the ministry of the Holy Spirit in our lives and in our relationships with others.

This was Jacob's problem. God wanted him to leave "at once." However, he evidently thought up methods that would enable him to make a transition. True, he tried to be "wise as a serpent and harmless as a dove"—as Jesus says we should be—but his approach did not consider God's direct exhortations.

Again, don't misunderstand. Methods that enable us to "make a transition" are not necessarily wrong methods. In fact, they may be great methods if this is what God wants. In Jacob's case, his methods were out of harmony with God's instructions.

Obviously, we're given much more freedom in decision making than Jacob. However, the principle still applies. With the freedom God has given us, we must make sure we select methods that are compatible with God's direct revelation in the Scriptures.

*Principle 2. When we make mistakes (functionally or methodologically) God sees our hearts and is able to sift the "grain from the chaff" and blesses us to the degree to which we're living up to the light we have.*

It's comforting to understand and believe this principle. It keeps us from the debilitating affects of persistent guilt and self-punishment. It helps us put the past behind us and go on and accept God's forgiveness.

On the other hand, comprehending this principle may lead us into dangerous waters. We're tempted to take advantage of God's grace and rationalize attitudes and actions that are out of God's will. We can tell ourselves that the end justifies the means. We can find ourselves in double trouble when the "end" is both something God wants and something *we* want to do for our own self-glorification and personal satisfaction.

*Principle 3. When we take matters into our own hands and use methods that are out of harmony with God's will, we will eventually experience negative consequences.*

This happened to Jacob. He tried to manipulate the situation for his own ends. And it intensified his problems with Laban. It made leaving a much more difficult process.

It's interesting that we often try to take "short cuts." By contrast, Jacob tried to "elongate" the process. But the principle applies either way. We should choose methods that do best what God wants. If we don't, we'll experience negative results. This does not mean that when we obediently do God's will we will not suffer. However, we'll be suffering for Christ, not because of our own mistakes. According to Peter, this is what brings honor to God (1 Pet. 2:19–20).

*Principle 4. If we are God's children, our loving heavenly Father will discipline us when we make mistakes, then help us return to our "Bethel experience."*

This happened in Jacob's life. God reminded him of his commitments and made it possible for him to maintain those commitments, even when he was floundering.

This also signals another caution. We must not interpret God's material blessings as a total approval of what we're doing. We may enjoy these blessings and suffer serious consequences in other areas of our lives.

Again this happened to Jacob. His greatest material prosperity came when he was trying to work things out on his own. At the same time, he suffered greatly in his family situation.

In conclusion, Jacob teaches us that the significant place to be is in the will of God in all respects, both in obeying his commandments and in the way we carry out those commands. Fortunately, we have the totality of God's revelation in the Scriptures and the personal presence of the Holy Spirit to enable us to walk worthy of our great calling. This is a great advantage over Jacob who lived in the midst of a pagan culture and at the same time only heard God's voice on rare occasions. This makes us far more responsible to live up to the light we have!

## Personalizing These Principles

The following questions will help you apply these principles to your life. Answer them as honestly as you can.

1. In what ways do I revert to my old ways of doing things that focus on the "wisdom of the world" rather than the "wisdom of God?"

2. In what ways have I operated with mixed motives—for example, honoring God and myself at the same time. Did God bless me? What can I do to keep my motives more pure?

3. What price have I had to pay for persistently doing things to honor myself rather than God?

4. How has God disciplined me when I've persistently put myself first rather than God?

## Set a Goal

As you reflect on the principles in this chapter, check those areas you feel good about in living the Christian life. Then, focus on the one principle you have the most difficulty applying. For example, you find yourself operating more as an opportunist than to glorify God. Whatever your need, write out a personal goal to be more pure in your motives:

_____

_____

_____

_____

_____

## Memorize the Following Scripture

*I have been crucified with Christ and I no longer live, but Christ lives in me. The life I live in the body, I live by faith in the Son of God, who loved me and gave himself for me.*
GALATIANS 2:20

## Growing Together

The following questions are designed for small-group discussion:

1. Is it possible to function with motives that are totally God-centered?

2. In the light of Philippians 2:3–4, how can we keep a proper balance in our motives? We do have our own interests, and Paul acknowledged that. But how can we keep them secondary and still survive, particularly in the business community?

3. How can we avoid "opportunism" and yet take advantage of "opportunities" for self-advancement that will glorify God?

4. What can we pray about for our own lives—as husbands, fathers and businessmen?

# Chapter 9

# *A Difficult Confrontation*
### Read Genesis 31:1–55

When Jacob left Bersheeba nearly twenty years earlier and headed for Haran, he had a major character flaw. He was deceptive!

But in spite of this weakness God had a special plan for his life—just as He had for his grandfather, Abraham, and his father, Isaac. They were to form the human chain through whom the Messiah would come to bring the gift of eternal salvation (Gen. 12:1–3).[1]

## *From "Pillow to Pillar"*

When Jacob left Bersheeba and headed for Haran, he was embarking on a painful journey that was orchestrated by the Lord to bring him face-to-face with himself and his character weakness. But before he could see himself as he really was, he needed to come "face-to-face" with God. This is what happened at Bethel, the first night on his journey to Haran. It was there he "met God," who revealed Himself to Jacob in a dream. Jacob was so overpowered by that experience that he cried out, "How awesome is this place! This is none other than the house of God; this is the gate of heaven" (28:17). It was then that he took the stone he had used as a pillow and "set it up as a pillar and poured oil on top of it" (28:18). He named the pillar Bethel, which means "house of God." It was there Jacob also promised God he'd give 10 percent of all his material possessions if God made it possible (28:22).

This was an important beginning point in Jacob's life in overcoming his character weakness—as it is in all of our lives. When we are born again and from God's eternal perspective enter "the gate of heaven," we embark on a spiritual journey in conforming our lives to Jesus Christ.

## Building Character

Like many of us who have character weaknesses of one sort or another when we embark on our own spiritual journey, Jacob didn't yet realize how serious his problem really was. Consequently, God designed a period of time to help Jacob see himself as he really was. Ironically, God used Jacob's Uncle Laban—a very dishonest and selfish man—to reflect Jacob's own character weakness.

For Jacob, it took twenty difficult and painful years to develop the qualities of honesty and integrity. His greatest insight into his own deceptive nature happened when Laban pulled the same trick on him that he had pulled on his father and his brother. When he looked at Laban, he saw himself and understood for the first time what it felt like to be on the receiving end of trickery.

Jacob learned from this experience. As we'll see, he demonstrated loyalty to his father-in-law in spite of the fact that Laban conned and deceived him, making Jacob take the brunt of his dishonesty. But God was watching and revealed Himself to Jacob and informed him that Laban's behavior had not gone unnoticed (31:12). It was then that God once again appeared to Jacob in a dream and said, "I am the God of Bethel, where you anointed a pillar and where you made a vow to me. Now leave this land at once and go back to your native land" (31:13).

## Prolonged Obedience

Unfortunately, Jacob wasn't listening as carefully as he should have been. God made it clear in this dream that he was to *leave immediately*. But, as we've seen in our last chapter, Jacob prolonged his stay for another six years. Working out a deal with his Uncle Laban, he allowed his own materialistic concerns to delay his leaving. Nevertheless, God blessed Jacob materially during this time. However, Laban and his whole family turned against him, and once again Jacob became the target of Laban's dishonesty. It was another painful six years.[2]

## Immediate Obedience

God once again appeared to Jacob at the end of this six-year period and reiterated His command to leave Haran. We read: "*Then* the Lord said to Jacob, 'Go back to the land of your fathers and to your relatives, and I will be with you'" (31:3).

This time Jacob heard *everything* God said. He knew he had to leave immediately, and he believed that God would protect him from anything that Laban might do to try to harm him.

## "Why Stay?"

Jacob shared God's revelation with Leah and Rachel. They agreed to leaving, but it's obvious their affirmation was based more on human factors than divine guidance (31:14–16). They concluded that they no longer had "any inheritance" and that their father treated them more like foreigners than family. It's obvious that they felt there was nothing to be gained by staying. Jacob had become far more wealthy than their father. Why not do what God told Jacob in his dream? If God really meant what He said in terms of protecting them, why stay?

It's important to understand that both Leah and Rachel at this point in their lives were not paragons of spiritual virtue. They were both products of a pagan and idolatrous culture. Their perspectives were far more materialistic than spiritual. In their carnal state, they did not comprehend what was happening in Jacob's life, let alone understand God's divine plan for the whole world. Had they grasped the significance of all this—and their part in it—they would have responded far differently. Their human thinking and logic would have been replaced with divine praise and thanksgiving.

## "Let's Go!"

Jacob must have breathed a sigh of relief when both Leah and Rachel agreed the time had come to leave. His fear began to dissipate. Furthermore, the circumstances seemed to be right. Laban was some distance away shearing his sheep. Consequently, "Jacob put his children and his wives on camels, and he drove all his livestock ahead of him, along with all the goods he had accumulated in Paddan Aram, to go to his father Isaac in the land of Canaan" (31:17–18).

To leave while Laban was away was, of course, deceptive. But at this point, Jacob's deception seems justified. His motives were right and pure. He was simply using common sense. Laban had demonstrated again and again he could not be trusted. To seek his permission could have put Jacob's whole family in jeopardy. At this point, he knew he had to "obey God rather than man." To prolong leaving would be to once again ignore God's command.

## Livid Laban

When Laban returned and discovered Jacob had left, he was livid. To add insult to injury, he discovered his "household gods" were missing (31:19). Unknown to him—and Jacob—his own daughter, Rachel, had taken them. His conclusion, of course, was that Jacob had stolen them. Consequently, he pursued Jacob and a week later, finally overtook him (31:22–23).

### A Divine Warning

Something happened that Laban did not anticipate. God also appeared to him in a dream and warned him not to harm Jacob—as Laban was obviously intent on doing (31:24, 29). The Lord was concerned about Jacob's safety. In fact, He had promised to protect him (31:3).

I believe God was also reaching out to Laban. After all, he was Jacob's uncle as well as his father-in-law. Furthermore, God loves all people. That was the primary reason He called Laban's uncle, Abraham, out of Ur of the Chaldeans and took him into the land of Canaan. If God could change Jacob—which He did—He could change Laban as well.

### A Change of Heart

Laban's "dream experience" grabbed his attention and helped him get a handle on his anger. Rather than act first and talk later, when Laban caught up with Jacob, he approached the situation with his usual suave demeanor. With an unusual blend of straightforward questions and statements as well as his typical hypocritical manipulation, he stated his case: "Then Laban said to Jacob, 'What have you done? You've *deceived me* [how ironic!], and you've carried off my daughters like captives in war. Why did you run off secretly and *deceive me* [how hypocritical!]? Why didn't you tell me, so I could send you away with joy and singing to the music of tambourines and harps [how manipulative!]? You didn't even let me kiss my grandchildren and my daughters good-bye. You have done a foolish thing'" (31:26–28).

In spite of his typical approach to human relationships, this is probably the most straightforward approach Laban had taken in a long time. The Lord had gotten his attention, which he made clear to Jacob when he said, "I have the power to harm you; but last night the God of your father said to me, 'Be careful not to say anything to Jacob, either good or bad'" (31:29).

There was, however, something that greatly puzzled Laban. He was having difficulty reconciling the fact that "the God" of Jacob's father, Isaac, was protecting him, and yet—in his mind—Jacob had stolen his pagan gods. If the God of Abraham and Isaac was on Jacob's side, why would he need Laban's pagan deities?

## Jacob's Two-fold Response

### "I Was Afraid!"

*First*, Jacob informed his father-in-law that he was afraid of him. He knew Laban had the power to harm him and to retrieve his daughters and Jacob's total estate—which had become far greater in value than Laban's.

### "See for Yourself!"

Laban's accusation upset Jacob. He resented being accused of taking Laban's household gods. Ironically, stealing and dishonesty had become a "character issue" with Jacob. He did not appreciate being accused of either, which is apparent in his response: "If you find anyone who has your gods, he shall not live. In the presence of our relatives, see for yourself whether there is anything of yours here with me; and if so, take it" (31:32).

## An Unknown Culprit

Jacob, of course, was totally unaware that his beloved Rachel was the culprit. Otherwise, he certainly wouldn't have put her life in jeopardy. However, Rachel quickly sensed the gravity of the situation and hurriedly devised a plan to deceive her father.

While Laban was looking through Leah's tent, Rachel removed the gods from her own living quarters and placed them in her camel's saddlebag and used the saddle as a seat. When Laban entered her tent, she quickly apologized for not standing up when he walked by, giving the excuse that she was menstruating. The plan worked because we read that "he searched but could not find the household gods" (31:35).

## What Goes Around Comes Around!

Though a very serious set of circumstances, one cannot help but smile. Laban had taught Rachel well! Like father, like daughter. She was just as deceptive as he was.

On the serious side, Rachel's behavior demonstrates her spiritual status. She was not a godly woman. She had not totally left her pagan ways—either in her worship practices or in her lifestyle. She was still polytheistic. Her father's "gods" were still her "gods." And Jacob's "God" was just another "god" in her life. Though she, along with Leah, had acknowledged that Jacob's "God" had spoken to him, she did not worship Him and Him alone. Though she had even prayed and received answers, she apparently felt she needed her father's gods as an additional security blanket.

There may also be other reasons why she stole them. She was probably still very angry at her dad for promising her to Jacob and then substituting Leah. She would never forget that event. How could she? The last thirteen years had been a painful experience. She had waited patiently for seven years to marry Jacob as her sole husband and lover. And then she discovered, because of her father's deceptive plot, that she had to share him with Leah—a persistent reminder of the emotional pain that goes along with every polygamous marriage. What better way to get even with her father than to steal what was most important to him! Perhaps in her own carnal mind, Rachel also may have believed she was helping "Jacob's God" by taking her "father's gods" with them as additional protection on this dangerous journey.

## Jacob's "Day in Court"

Whatever Rachel's motives, God protected Jacob in the midst of what could have become a disastrous development. Had Laban found his gods, who knows what he might have done? In his ignorance, Jacob seized the moment to vent his own anger. For the first time in twenty years, he defended his own character—something he could never have done prior to his Bethel experience. Though Jacob was far from what God wanted him to be spiritually, he had come a long way in overcoming his character weakness. To be falsely accused in view of his loyalty to a man who had deceived him numerous times over the years was all that Jacob needed to ignite the feelings of resentment that had built up over the years. To be more specific, the biblical record states that "Jacob was *angry* and took Laban to task" (31:36).

In the presence of the extended family—all of Laban's sons were no doubt there—Jacob had his own day in court! "What is my crime?" he asked Laban. "What sin have I committed that you hunt me down?" (31:36).

## Evidence That Demands a Verdict

Jacob followed his pointed questions with some very substantial evidence. The biblical record speaks for itself and testifies to Jacob's loyalty, honesty, and perseverance in the midst of a very difficult situation:

> I have been with you for twenty years now. Your sheep and goats have not miscarried, nor have I eaten rams from your flocks. I did not bring you animals torn by wild beasts; I bore the loss myself. And you demanded payment from me for whatever was stolen by day or night. This was my situation: The heat consumed me in the daytime and the cold at night, and sleep fled from my eyes. It was like this for the twenty years I was in your household. I worked for you fourteen years for your two daughters and six years for your flocks, and you changed my wages ten times. If the God of my father, the God of Abraham and the fear of Isaac, had not been with me, you would surely have sent me away empty-handed. But God has seen my hardship and the toil of my hands, and last night he rebuked you. (Gen. 31:38–42)

There's intense emotion in this speech! Jacob was clearly offended. He believed he had paid his dues, and indeed he had. Though he was not *the man he could be*, he was not *the man he was* when he deceived his father and his brother twenty years before.

The biblical record confirms that Jacob was not using false information to build his case. This is why God told him in His initial revelation that He had seen all that Laban had been doing (31:12). This was evidence that demanded a verdict in Jacob's favor. Laban was guilty of incredible manipulation, selfishness, deception and insensitivity.

## *No Leg to Stand on, But . . .*

Though Laban tried another manipulative tactic, his response attests to Jacob's honesty. He could not—and did not—contradict what Jacob had said. He knew it was the truth—and so did everyone in the family who was listening to everything that Jacob had said.

Even though Laban's response was conciliatory, it was still manipulative. He appealed to the fact that his daughters were involved and that he had family ties with Jacob's children. He also reminded Jacob that he came to him with nothing, and without his sheep and goats, Jacob would have nothing. In fact, he gestured that the sheep and goats in Jacob's great flock were *his* flocks. More specifically, he said, "All you see is mine" (31:43). In actuality, with this statement, Laban had just changed Jacob's wages an eleventh time. His attitude and behavior had begun to change, but his own sinful character weaknesses—selfishness and dishonesty—raised their ugly heads. The fact is he didn't have a leg to stand on. Nevertheless, he tried one more time to put Jacob on a guilt trip!

But down deep in his heart, Laban knew he *had* mistreated Jacob—and everyone in his family knew it. Consequently, he proposed a truce. "Come now," he said, "let's make a covenant, you and I, and let it serve as a witness between us" (31:44).

## The Tide Had Turned

Jacob responded immediately and took control. He had been down this road before. The biblical record reads that Jacob "took a stone and set it up as a pillar," and he said to his relatives, "'gather some stones'" (31:45–46).

Wisely, Jacob involved the whole family in this truce, which probably included Laban's sons as well as his daughters, Leah and Rachel. It was they who "took stones and piled them in a heap," and it was "they" who "ate there by the heap" (31:46). Laban used an Aramaic phrase, "Jegar Sahadutha," to describe the altar. Jacob used a Hebrew word, "Galeed," to describe the same altar. Both concepts, however, identify the stones as a "witness heap" (31:47).

## Could This Be Laban?

For the first time in twenty years, Laban seemed honest and sincere. Could it be that this was *his* "Bethel experience"—that he knew in his heart that God in His grace had reached out to him in a dream just as He had reached out to Jacob? Though his response was not overly warm and cordial, it demonstrates that Laban knew Jacob was not asking for something unfair. The fact that he did not defend his actions when Jacob opened his heart points to the fact that he had no recourse but to suggest a truce and release his son-in-law without harming him or his family.

Two important statements stand out in the agreement proposed by Laban. First, he said, "May the Lord keep watch between you and me when we are away from each other" (31:49).

Out of context this sounds like a very spiritual, friendly, and trusting statement. However, it is worded so as to remind Jacob that this God he trusts and serves is watching his every movement and action, and if he ever mistreats Leah and Rachel, then that God has the right to judge and discipline him. The agreement certainly puts the onus and responsibility on Jacob. In other words, if God is the God Jacob says He is, he had better watch his every step.

Furthermore, from this point forward in the dialogue, Laban focused the conversation *on God.* If he's being honest—which it appears he is—Laban seems to have taken a very important step in his spiritual life, acknowledging that God is indeed the one true God, "the God of Abraham and the God of Nahor" (31:53).

The second agreement in the contract is more pragmatic and one that can be monitored by every member of the family: "This heap is a witness, and this pillar is a witness, that I will not go past this heap to your side to harm you and that you will not go past this heap and pillar to my side to harm me" (31:52).

## *The Line Is Drawn*

Jacob quickly endorsed these agreements, again demonstrating his honesty and his integrity. He had nothing to lose and everything to gain. He was committed to Rachel and Leah—something he had demonstrated ever since Laban had tricked him. Furthermore, he had no intentions of hurting Laban or taking advantage of him—again something he had demonstrated for twenty years. Consequently, Jacob "offered a sacrifice there in the hill country and invited his relatives to a meal" (31:54).

The next morning, these two men separated. Laban and his family returned to Haran, and Jacob continued his journey to his homeland, bringing with him his wives, his children, and all the servants and animals he had accumulated. Though there was little love lost between these two men, they went their separate ways and, as far as we know, never met again on this earth.

Hopefully, these two men met again in heaven. There's no question about Jacob's eternal salvation. His Bethel experience was real. Only God knows what eventually happened to Laban. One thing is sure. He had every opportunity to come to know the God of Abraham, Isaac, and Jacob in a personal way. Perhaps this was a "change point" that launched him on a dynamic spiritual journey.

## Becoming God's Man Today

*Principles to Live By*

### Principle 1. Overcoming character weaknesses is usually a process that takes both time and some painful experiences— even for Christians.

I've seen this in my own life. I grew up in a religious and ethnic community that was permeated with prejudice. I didn't even realize how deeply this thinking had penetrated my soul and had become a part of the fabric of my personality. It took nearly five years to purge me of this insidious sin.

About two years into this learning experience, God pulled the rug out from under me, allowing me to flounder in disillusionment. I had to reach up to touch bottom. In the process, I had to look to those who I felt were my inferiors spiritually. It was they who reached out a hand to help me once again stand on my own two feet. But this time, I had my feet more firmly planted on God's grace in my life rather than on my works-oriented religious background.

God took five years to deal with Peter's Jewish prejudice. It took a vision from heaven to convince him that Jesus Christ came to die for Gentiles as well as Jews (Acts 10). If it took that much time for a man who literally walked with Jesus, heard Him teach, and saw Him crucified and resurrected, it shouldn't surprise us that it takes time to deal with our character weaknesses as well.

### Principle 2. God designs experiences and utilizes events and circumstances to uncover our character weaknesses and to assist us in overcoming those weaknesses.

God never pulls the rug out from under us just to see us flounder. He does not delight in just hurting us. Rather, He designs these wilderness experiences to help us grow and mature.

This is what He did in Jacob's life. This is also what He did in Moses' life when he had to flee for his life from Egypt. God was preparing this great prophet for the superhuman task of leading the children of Israel out of Egypt.

I now see clearly that this was what God was doing in my own life. Unfortunately, it often takes experiences like these to get our attention—to get us to listen. If it's only words of exhortation, they seem to go in one ear and out the other. Can you identify with this kind of experience?

*Principle 3. God gives those who have overcome character weaknesses natural opportunities to demonstrate before others the reality of what has happened in their lives.*

Jacob certainly had this opportunity when he confronted Laban. And as we'll see, he had future opportunities to demonstrate his faith before his whole family.

As I write these words, it has suddenly dawned on me that God has given me an opportunity to share my experience with you. I hope you will be able to identify with some character weakness in your own life and perhaps change before you have a disciplinary crisis that will be far more painful than discovering that a character weakness exists in your life. Truth, of course, is painful—but a crisis experience to help you deal with that truth is even more painful.

*Principle 4. God uses our personal journeys in overcoming character weaknesses to assist others in overcoming their weaknesses—even those who may have used our weaknesses for their own selfish purposes.*

Have you ever had someone take advantage of your character weakness in order to further their own selfish goals? I have. For example, my tendency is to fear confronting people because of my own fear of rejection. Though much of my hesitancy to confront also relates to the fact that I don't like to hurt people, if I'm really honest, I don't like people to dislike me.

On several occasions, people have used this weakness in my life to feather their own nest and to take advantage of me. I remember one particular situation. I set the stage for this man's success. I believed in him and supported him. And then I began to realize that he was taking advantage of my trust. While I was building him up, he was subtly tearing me down!

When I saw what was happening, I knew what I had to do. If I really loved this man, I could not allow him to continue to take advantage of others. I had to tell the truth—which I did. Though there were a number of factors that brought his world crashing down, it began when I spoke out, without anger and retaliation, and unveiled this man's motivations.

Later, when he was in a terrible state of pain and disillusionment because of his manipulative behavior in several other situations, I was the one that was able to reach out a helping hand. How could I do otherwise when God has been so gracious to me when I've been in a state of disillusionment because of my own character weaknesses?

*Principle 5. God desires to ultimately deliver us from our difficult situations and to provide us with a new start in life.*

It's never too late to start over. Though we certainly cannot change some things in the past, we can stop blaming ourselves and move forward. We need not punish ourselves and be in bondage to guilt. God wants to take our weaknesses and use them as strengths in the future. As we'll see, this is certainly what He did with Jacob.

## Personalizing These Principles

Use the following questions to reflect on your own life as a Christian.

1. Have I accepted the fact that overcoming character weaknesses is a process that often takes time and pain?

2. Am I able to see uncomfortable circumstances as an opportunity to grow in my Christian life?

3. Am I able to imagine the opportunities God may provide for me to share with others how God has helped me to overcome character weaknesses?

4. Is there someone I know who has taken advantage of my weaknesses that I might be able to help overcome his or her weaknesses?

5. Do I really understand what it means to be a new creation in Christ—no matter what has happened in the past?

### Set a Goal

As you reflect on the principles in this chapter, can you identify one of these principles that is particularly applicable to your life right now?

For example, you may have overcome a character weakness, but you've not taken the opportunity to help another brother in Christ overcome the same or similar weakness. Set a goal for your life that will help you apply the principle you've chosen.

_____

_____

_____

_____

_____

## Memorize the Following Scripture

> *For this very reason, make every effort to add to your faith goodness; and to goodness, knowledge; and to knowledge, self-control; and to self-control, perseverance; and to perseverance, godliness; and to godliness, brotherly kindness; and to brotherly kindness, love. For if you possess these qualities in increasing measure, they will keep you from being ineffective and unproductive in your knowledge of our Lord Jesus Christ.*
>                                    2 PETER 1:5–8

## Growing Together

The following questions are designed for small-group discussion:

1. How has God enabled you to overcome a character weakness? What was the process He used in your life?

2. Most of us are somewhere in the process of overcoming a character weakness. Would you feel free to share with us what God is doing in your life at the present time?

3. How have you been able to help others to overcome their character weaknesses because of the way in which God has helped you?

4. What specific prayer need can you share with each of us so that we can pray for one another?

Chapter 10

# Solving Problems God's Way
### Read Genesis 32:1–21

*I* remember on one occasion facing a challenge in the ministry that seemingly had no solution—at least not a solution that would be fair and right. In this instance, no matter what steps I took, it seemed that the problem got more complex. I had to face the fact that I had no appropriate solution—and I could not think of one.

## Wisdom from Above

Then I shared the problem with a group of mature Christian men who served with me. I shared my frustration and my anxiety, and I admitted that I didn't know what to do. Not surprisingly, they didn't have an immediate solution either. But as we talked and prayed, we knew we had to do something to resolve the problem—but we still didn't know how. Suddenly, I awakened one morning with a creative solution that none of us had thought about—a solution that seemed to resolve all aspects of the problem. As I shared this idea, everyone who had been trying to come up with a solution immediately saw that this was indeed what we should do. God had answered our prayers.

Most of us face challenges in our lives when there doesn't seem to be a positive solution. Unfortunately, it's easy to take matters into our own hands, relying on our own ingenuity and trying to make the best of a bad situation. There is, of course, another dimension to this kind of challenge. Though God wants us to use the brain He's given us, He doesn't want us to "lean on our own understanding." He wants to be a unique part of the solution. He desires to provide us with divine wisdom (James 1:5).

As we'll see in this chapter, this was a lesson Jacob was learning, and it's a lesson all of us need to learn as well.

## *An Encounter of a Different Kind*

After separating from Laban and continuing his journey back to his homeland, Jacob met "the angels of God" (Gen. 32:1). This is an identical description of the heavenly messengers Jacob saw in his dream at Bethel twenty years earlier. At that time, they were "ascending and descending" on a stairway or ladder that extended from earth to heaven. The difference in this second appearance, however, is that they visibly appeared to Jacob when his eyes were wide open. It was not a dream nor a figment of his imagination. Rather, it was a face-to-face encounter.

### God's Invisible World Touched Jacob's Visible World

Though these two events are the only time this particular phrase—"the angels of God"—is used in the Old Testament, it is not the only time God's "invisible world" clearly touched our "visible world." God periodically communicated with His people in this way, particularly during the time He was reaching out to a lost and pagan society during the days of Abraham and Isaac (Gen. 16:7; 18:1; 19:1; 22:11). God was continuing to use this means to communicate His will to Jacob.

### A Divine Connection

More specifically, God was reassuring Jacob that He was with him as He had promised He would be (31:3). Jacob was obviously encouraged by this angelic appearance. He couldn't miss the connection between this supernatural encounter and his experience at Bethel twenty years before. After all, when God initially told him to leave Laban, He let Jacob know that He was indeed "the God of Bethel" (31:13).

At this moment, Jacob clearly understood what God was doing. As he changed the name of that place two decades before from "Luz" to "Bethel"—meaning "house of God"—(28:19), Jacob now named this place Mahanaim, which means "two" (32:2). Jacob was apparently referring to the fact that there were *two* "angels of God."

## "Leaving" and "Returning"

There is another important correlation between these two events. When God communicated with Jacob at Bethel, he was *leaving* his homeland. When God communicated with him at Mahanaim, Jacob was *returning*. The Holy Spirit definitely wants us to see a significant relationship between these two events—just as He wanted Jacob to see this connection.

## Testing the Waters

Uppermost in Jacob's thoughts was the challenge to rebuild the relationship with his brother, Esau. The last time he saw him, Esau was so angry he was contemplating murder. Though years had passed, Jacob knew that this kind of resentment has a way of lingering and residing just below the surface. Furthermore, he still had vivid recollections of Esau's volatile personality. Even decades do not erase such memories. What would happen when they met each other?

### Taking No Chances!

To test the waters, Jacob "sent messengers ahead of him" to meet his brother (32:3). He also gave them very specific instructions: "This is what you are to say to my *master* Esau: 'Your *servant* Jacob says, I have been staying with Laban and have remained there till now. I have cattle and donkeys, sheep and goats, menservants and maidservants. Now I am sending this message to *my lord*, that I might find favor in your eyes'" (32:4–5).

### A "Role Reversal"

Jacob's message to Esau indicates that he also had vivid memories of what he had done to Esau. He had made himself "lord" over Esau in a deceptive way and at the same time had made his brother his "servant." In Jacob's message to Esau, he reversed these roles, hoping to pacify his brother and to make amends. Thus he placed himself in a "servant" role to Esau and called him his "lord."

Jacob also wanted Esau to know that he would pay for his sin with "cattle and donkeys, sheep and goats, menservants and maidservants." He was willing to use his resources to buy Esau's forgiveness.

We must remind ourselves that God had predetermined before the boys were ever born that Esau would serve Jacob (25:23). However, this did not justify Jacob's deception and manipulation. God didn't need Jacob's help, and He certainly rejected the way he went about securing what belonged to him by divine decree. What Jacob did was very wrong, and he knew it! After meeting God at Bethel, he began to face his sinful attitudes and actions.

## Old Habits Are Hard to Change

Though Jacob began to see himself as he really was when he encountered "the angels of God" at Bethel, it took a face-to-face encounter with Laban—a man just like him—to help him break away from his old habits. Though it took a painful twenty years, it was a character building experience.

But since old habits are hard to change, we see Jacob regressing by taking matters into his own hands and "testing the waters." Though it certainly wasn't wrong for Jacob to plan ahead and think through the issues, he was not responding to God's reassurances. He had more lessons to learn. And, as He usually does, God allowed Jacob to learn these lessons.

## Wrong Perceptions

Evidently, Jacob's emissaries never even got close enough to talk with Esau. As they approached the "land of Seir" where Esau resided, they were astonished to see four hundred men advancing towards them. Staying around just long enough to conclude that they had encountered Esau's personal "army," they turned and hightailed it back to report to Jacob what they had seen (32:6).

Jacob was astonished! His fear turned to paranoia. Not knowing this report was erroneous, he concluded that Esau was still angry and still had plans to kill him. Motivated by intense "fear and distress," he "divided the people who were with him into two groups." In his panic, he devised a scheme to save at least some of his family and his servants, as well as some of his flocks and herds and camels. He reasoned that if Esau attacked one group, the others would at least have a chance to escape (33:7–8).

## Logical Questions

Why didn't Jacob turn to the Lord with his concerns about Esau, even before he sent messengers to meet him? After all, he had several recent and direct reassurances that God was with him:

➤ a direct revelation from God telling him to leave (31:3)

➤ God's previous protection by appearing to Laban in a dream (31:24)

➤ a face-to-face encounter with "the angels of God" (32:1)

Why didn't Jacob consult God for wisdom? The answer seems clear and it is one that most of us can identify with: how quickly we revert to our old ways of doing things! Old patterns and habits are hard to break. Our memories fade so quickly, particularly when we get into difficult situations. We believe we can resolve the problem on our own. We take matters into our own hands. We "lean on our own understanding." Fear drives us to rely on our natural instincts.

## When All Else Fails, Pray!

Eventually, Jacob turned to God for help (Gen. 32:9–12). However, it happened after he had no human recourse. He saw no way out. He felt doomed!

How typical of many of us today. As long as we think we can handle problems ourselves, we devise our own schemes and leave God out of the picture. Though we believe in Him and we know in our hearts He is with us, we don't consult Him as we should *until* we get ourselves into a predicament that overwhelms us.

That's exactly what happened to Jacob. Actually, his prayer is a "model" prayer, even though he should have used this divine resource earlier.

### "God, You Are God"

This is a divine pattern in many biblical prayers—to acknowledge who God really is! When Nehemiah prayed about the sad condition of his people in Jerusalem, he lifted his voice to God and said, "Oh Lord, God of Heaven, the great and awesome God" (Neh. 1:5). When Jesus taught His disciples to pray, He said, "This, then, is how you should pray: 'Our Father in heaven, hallowed be your name, . . .'" (Matt. 6:9).

Jacob addressed the Lord as the God of his "father Abraham" and his "father Isaac" (Gen. 32:9a). This is significant. He was beginning to understand more fully his place in God's divine plan. Though he was not yet the man God wanted him to be, he was moving in the right direction. Though he had waited too long to consult God about the crisis he was facing, he at least didn't try to arm himself for battle against his brother. That would have been the "old Jacob"—the Jacob of "pre-Bethel" days.

## God, You Promised

After acknowledging who God was, and that it was He who had called Abraham out of Ur of the Chaldeans and miraculously caused Sarah to give birth to Isaac, Jacob reminded the Lord of what He had told him specifically in his various revelations—that it was He, the Lord, who had said, "Go back to your country and your relatives." He also reminded the Lord that it was He who had said, "I will make you prosper" (32:9b).

With this prayer, Jacob was also reminding the Lord that he understood the promise God had made to Abraham. Though he was still in the process of grasping his unique place in this divine plan, Jacob understood it well enough to know that God had promised to be with him in a special way, enabling him to fulfill his part in the Abrahamic covenant. Though his thoughts at this moment were definitely more focused on personal protection, material prosperity, and family multiplication, he was responding to what he was able to grasp at this point in his spiritual development.

## God, I'm Unworthy

Jacob's prayer demonstrates where he was in his spiritual journey. Though he was still operating at a very human level, he knew God had blessed him and had taken care of him, even though he had deceived his father and stolen the birthright and blessing from Esau. Thus, as never before, he humbled himself before God and cried out, "I am unworthy of all the kindness and faithfulness you have shown your servant. I had only my staff when I crossed this Jordan, but now I have become two groups" (32:10).

## God, Please Help Me

In the next part of his prayer, Jacob let God know exactly what he was feeling and what he needed. Thus he prayed, "Save me, I pray, from the hand of my brother Esau, for I am afraid he will come and attack me, and also the mothers with their children" (32:11).

These words in Jacob's prayer reveal another character quality that God was developing in Jacob's life. He was not only concerned for himself; he was deeply concerned for his family and his servants. He thought Esau was armed for battle with four hundred men, and if they attacked, he knew it could be a massacre. It was not uncommon in those days for whole families to be wiped out by an enemy attack, including women, children, and servants.

This part of Jacob's prayer also helps us understand his deep sense of fear and anxiety. This was a life and death crisis. There was no way he could humanly protect himself and his whole household against this kind of onslaught. They would be open targets. There was no place to hide. In that sense, his back was against the wall.

### God, Please Remember—You Promised

Jacob concluded his prayer with a statement that reveals that he knew very specifically what God had promised his grandfather, Abraham, and his father, Isaac. What he shared with the Lord at this moment was a direct correlation with the covenant God made when He chose Abraham out of Ur of the Chaldeans. Thus we read: "But you have said, 'I will surely make you prosper and will make your descendants like the sand of the sea, which cannot be counted'" (32:12).

When did Jacob hear about this specific aspect of God's promise to Abraham? Surely he remembered hearing his father share the incredible story when God asked Abraham to offer his father, Isaac, as a sacrifice on Mount Moriah. Both he and Esau must have heard this story many times. Isaac would never forget what God said after He had provided a ram and saved his life: "I will surely bless you and make your descendants as numerous as the stars in the sky and as the sands on the seashore" (22:17). In other words, Jacob heard these very words from his father's lips. And being out in the wilderness about ready to face total annihilation actually helped him remember the specific promise.

## Preparing for a "Desert Storm"

Perhaps as a test of Jacob's faith, God did not respond directly to Jacob's prayer. And still overwhelmed with what he believed was impending doom, Jacob didn't wait for the Lord's answer. He continued to develop a plan to avert what he firmly believed was a forthcoming disaster.

### A Gift That Would Multiply

Jacob prepared a gift for Esau—a total of 550 male and female animals (32:13–15). Jacob hopefully thought that Esau would be impressed with the proportion of females to males. The potential for rapid multiplication was obvious:

➤ 200 female goats, 20 male goats

➤ 200 ewes, 20 rams

➤ 30 female camels with their young

➤ 40 cows, 10 bulls

➤ 20 female donkeys, 10 male donkeys

## More Ingenuity!

Jacob also devised an ingenious plan to help his brother mentally absorb the magnitude of this gift. At the same time, he hoped the plan would pacify Esau and diffuse his anger.

Jacob arranged to have space between each herd. Esau would first encounter a herd of goats, giving him time to reflect on what was happening. Then, he would encounter a flock of sheep, followed by a herd of camels, cows, and donkeys. Each time that Esau would ask who owned the flocks and herds, Jacob's servants were to respond, "They belong to your *servant* Jacob. They are a gift sent to my *lord* Esau, and he is coming behind us" (32:18).

Jacob's strategy *was* ingenious. And since he did not have a direct word from the Lord as to how to solve the problem, he determined in his heart that he was going to face Esau. Thus he stated these final words to his servants as each flock or herd headed out: "Be sure to say, 'Your servant Jacob is coming behind us.' For he thought, 'I will pacify him with these gifts I am sending on ahead; later, when I see him, perhaps he will receive me'" (32:20).

Jacob was not certain of the outcome. But the die was cast. There was no turning back. I'm sure he was hoping against hope that God would answer his prayer and have mercy on him and his whole family. But in his mind, he couldn't wait for that assurance.

## *Was Jacob Wrong?*

Should Jacob have simply waited for God to protect him when Esau and his four hundred men arrived on the scene? The fact is, Esau was *not* angry (33:4). He had already forgiven Jacob. All of this anguish, fear, and distress was unnecessary—and for naught. Think of the trauma he unnecessarily created for himself and his whole family.

It's difficult to fault Jacob for his actions since God wants us to use our minds and our skills to solve our problems. But He also wants us to first and foremost rely on Him and to draw on His strength and wisdom. I believe Jacob should have waited for God to solve the problem. Think of the opportunity he had to demonstrate to his family that God really was God and that He had promised to be with him and his whole family. The angelic appearances should have reassured Jacob. If Esau were still angry, God could have easily intercepted him and his four hundred men just as He had recently intercepted Laban when He warned him in a dream not to harm Jacob.

However, let's give credit where credit is due. Jacob *was growing* in his faith. God was not finished with him yet. Before he even met Esau, something else happened to help him take another step in his spiritual development. He was going to meet God "face-to-face"—and from that point forward he would never be the same again. It would be the greatest "change point" in his life!

## Becoming God's Man Today

*Principles to Live By*

**Principle 1. God will never leave us or forsake us once we come to know Him personally through Jesus Christ— our initial "Bethel experience."**

This is one of the most reassuring lessons from Jacob's life story. God never forsook Jacob, even when he made serious mistakes and regressed to his old "flesh patterns." And God will not forsake us. Once we are "in Christ," we are His forever. The Holy Spirit is the "seal" and "a deposit guaranteeing our inheritance" (Eph. 1:13–14). No one can remove us from Christ's ultimate protection. Even our greatest mistakes and sins will not separate us from God's eternal love. Paul believed this truth and taught it with great conviction. He was absolutely sure that *nothing* "will be able to separate us from the love of God that is in Christ Jesus our Lord" (Rom. 8:39).

### A Wonderful Experience

I did not always believe in the security of my salvation. The first years of my life as a Christian were frustrating and difficult simply because I didn't have the assurance of my salvation. I was definitely saved, but I didn't know how secure I was in Jesus Christ. What a change took place in my day-to-day experience once I accepted and believed this great truth. My "roller coaster" life as a believer disappeared. I stopped relying on feelings and put my faith in the facts of God's eternal Word. This was one of the greatest "change points" in my own life.

## Meeting Our Material Needs

This truth also applies to the very pragmatic aspects of life—such as making a living. The author of Hebrews stated, "Keep your lives free from the love of money and be content with what you have, because God has said, 'Never will I leave you; never will I forsake you'" (Heb. 13:5). This is why Paul also wrote to the Philippians—"And my God will meet all your needs according to his glorious riches in Christ Jesus" (Phil. 4:19).

This, of course, is not an excuse for being irresponsible in working hard to make a living. In fact, Paul had no patience with lazy men. Writing to the Thessalonians, he said, "If a man will not work, he shall not eat" (2 Thess. 3:10). But here too is a balance. Jesus warned about being anxious about making a living, reminding all of us that if our heavenly Father is concerned about sparrows that fall and the flowers of the field, He is certainly concerned for us! (Matt. 6:25–34).

*Principle 2. God desires to transform us into His image and to use us to carry out His purposes in the world; however, the degree to which this happens depends on our willingness to follow Him and obey Him.*

God had a special purpose for Jacob. He was a very important link in God's eternal and divine plan to give birth to His chosen people, Israel, and to bring the Messiah into the world to be the Savior of all who believe.

However, God also has a special plan for all of us—to glorify God as His chosen people (Eph. 1:3–14). As believers we are members of the church, His body. The extent to which we will carry out that purpose depends on our commitment to Him.

Paul captured this truth beautifully when he wrote to the Romans: "Therefore, I urge you, brothers, in view of God's mercy, to offer your bodies as living sacrifices, holy and pleasing to God—which is your spiritual worship. Do not conform any longer to the pattern of this world, but *be transformed* by the renewing of your mind. Then you will be able to test and approve what God's will is—his good, pleasing and perfect will" (Rom. 12:1–2).

The degree to which we are able to truly prove what God's will is for us is the degree to which we are transformed into Christ's image by the "renewing of our minds." This happens when we think on those things that are true, noble, right, pure, lovely, admirable, and excellent (Phil. 4:8).

*Principle 3. God responds to faith in Himself and His Word and when we trust Him, He will "direct our paths."*

The Book of Proverbs succinctly summarizes this principle. We're told: "Trust in the Lord with all your heart and lean not on your own understanding; in all your ways acknowledge him, and he will make your paths straight" (Prov. 3:5–6).

When I first became a Christian, I wrote this proverb in the flyleaf of my Bible. Along with Romans 12:1–2, these verses became my favorites—my life verses. Though I don't always practice these great truths, I go back to them again and again, particularly when I revert or regress to my old "flesh patterns" in solving problems when facing the challenges of life.

I realize that God wants me to use my abilities to think and act in order to be a responsible human being. But I also realize that I'm not to "lean on" those God-given capabilities. I'm to lean on the Lord. I'm to trust Him! I'm to acknowledge that He is God and it is He who wants to direct my paths.

*Principle 4. God understands each of us and designs a "growth curriculum" that takes into consideration both our strengths and weaknesses.*

This is the most awesome part of God's great educational process. He wants to work with each of us individually. He has no standardized tests or lessons. Every step He leads us along the way is unique for each of us. How we respond to His leadership, however, determines whether or not we pass or fail in doing the perfect will of God.

What is even more exciting is that when we "fail" His tests, we always get another chance. In His scheme of things, "failure" becomes a means for growth and advancement. If we abide by His rules, we will never fail ultimately. We'll simply take another step in measuring up to the stature of the fullness of Jesus Christ (Eph. 4:13).

I remember preparing for my final doctoral exam at New York University. I was scared to death. To fail might mean nine years of hard work down the drain. Passing this exam was not "a learning experience" that would be just another step in getting my Ph.D. It was one of the final steps to measure whether or not I was qualified for this honor. Fortunately, I passed, but not without a lot of fear, anxiety, and hard work.

God does not evaluate our success or failure with this kind of absolute standard. We can always forget the past and press on for the prize that awaits us. As a Christian, it's never too late to retake God's tests.

*Principle 5. When crying out to God, He responds to prayer that comes from a sincere heart, even though we may have created the crisis because of our regression to our old "flesh patterns" that are more self-centered than God-centered (Phil. 4:6–7).*

We should never hesitate to approach God for help, even when we "mess up" in our spiritual journey. In fact, it's prayer that helps us get back in focus. It's seeking God's wisdom that helps us maintain that intricate balance between using our God-given capabilities and relying on God's supernatural guidance and strength.

We always need to remind ourselves of the words of Paul to the Philippians: "Do not be anxious about anything, but in everything, by prayer and petition, with thanksgiving, present your requests to God. And the peace of God, which transcends all understanding, will guard your hearts and your minds in Christ Jesus" (Phil. 4:6–7).

## Personalizing These Principles

Use the following questions to reflect on your own life as a Christian.

1. Do I have a day-by-day assurance of my personal salvation? If you cannot answer this question positively, consult the Scriptures outlined under the first principle on page 165. Also, read through the first eleven chapters of Paul's letter to the Romans, and note God's eternal and sovereign plan for all who truly believe in Jesus Christ for personal salvation.

2. Have I presented my body to Jesus Christ to be a living sacrifice? Am I conforming my life to the life of Christ by renewing my mind and heart with God's truth?

If you cannot answer these questions positively, read Romans chapters 12–16. Here Paul outlines specifically how to "renew our minds" and discover the good acceptable and perfect will of God.

3. Am I trusting God moment by moment, realizing that He wants to lead me to do those things that please Him? Do I really understand the great truths outlined in Proverbs 3:5–6?

4. Do I believe that God has a plan for my personal spiritual growth—one designed just for me? To what extent am I responding to His leadership and direction in my life?

5. When I face a crisis in my life, do I seek God's wisdom and help? Better yet, do I pray regularly for guidance, even when things are going well?

## Set a Goal

Which of the principles outlined in this chapter challenges you the most? For example, you may hesitate to ask God for help in a difficult situation because you've not been living in His will. You're ashamed and embarrassed. You may need to set a goal to pray regularly and seek His help—even though you've walked out of God's will or tried to solve life's problems in your own strength:

_____

_____

_____

_____

## Memorize the Following Scripture

*Trust in the Lord with all your heart and lean not on your own understanding; in all your ways acknowledge him, and he will make your paths straight.*

PROVERBS 3:5–6

## Growing Together

The following questions are designed for small group discussion:

1. Relative to having assurance of our salvation, have any of you had an experience similar to the author's which he shared on page 165? How did you come to the place where you felt secure in Christ?

2. There are sincere Christians who differ on the doctrine of "eternal security." If you do not believe this doctrine which some call "once

saved, always saved," share what you do in order to have a day-by-day sense of security that God will never leave you or forsake you. What is your explanation of Romans 8:28–39 and Ephesians 1:13–14?

Note: Try to not get bogged down with this question. Sincere Christians have disagreed on this issue for centuries. The important point is that we have the assurance of our salvation and that we're not relying on works to save us or to keep us saved.

3. How have you experienced God's day-to-day guidance in your life? How do you handle situations that don't seem to have human solutions?

4. What kind of "growth curriculum" has God designed for your life thus far in your Christian experience? Would you feel free to share how this learning experience is uniquely suited to your strengths and weaknesses?

5. What are some difficult challenges in your life right now that you can share with us so that we can all pray for you?

# Chapter 11

## *Wrestling with God*
### Read Genesis 32:22–32

*H*ave you ever had a sleepless night? I have—particularly when I'm worried about something. I can't recall the number of times I've suddenly awakened somewhere between 2:00 and 5:00 in the morning, unable to go back to sleep. My mind has been working overtime trying to solve some problem even in its unconscious state.

This is a reality for most of us. Even though we've attempted to trust God for the solution, we can't seem to let go of the struggle and at least wait until morning to continue to seek a solution.

I've learned one thing, however. When this happens, I have learned to increasingly rely on Paul's words to the Philippians: "Do not be anxious about anything, but in everything, by prayer and petition, with thanksgiving, present your requests to God. And the peace of God, which transcends all understanding, will guard your hearts and your minds in Christ Jesus" (Phil. 4:6–7).

As I've meditated on these verses, I have then prayed that God would help me to believe what Paul wrote. And guess what? When I sincerely follow this plan, I've often fallen soundly asleep, getting my needed rest.

On several occasions, my wife has awakened too—probably because I've been tossing and turning. I've shared with her my anxiety and why I felt this way. She has simply touched my back or taken my hand in hers and prayed Paul's prayer for me. While she's praying, I've actually felt the anxiety melt away, enabling me to once again go back to sleep. Unfortunately, I simply don't take God's Word as seriously as I should and as often as I should in order to be at peace, no matter what my struggles.

## Jacob's Sleepless Night

Jacob had prepared himself for the unknown. He knew he had to face Esau, no matter what the consequences. Even though he may have saved himself and his family a lot of anxiety by waiting on God to solve the problem, he still took a bold step of faith. He had no idea what the outcome would be!

That very night we read that he "got up and took his two wives, his two maidservants and his eleven sons and crossed the ford of the Jabbok" (Gen. 32:22). The fact that Jacob "got up" indicates he had already gone to bed. Questions must have been flooding his mind. Would Esau accept his gift? What if he didn't? What should he do next?

No doubt, unable to sleep, he awakened his family members and ushered them across the river. Next, he instructed his servants to transport all his possessions across, which would include all of his remaining livestock, his tents, and whatever other belongings he brought out of Mesopotamia.

## Jacob Crosses Jabbok

Crossing the river Jabbok seems symbolic in Jacob's life. First, the Hebrew words "Jacob" and "Jabbok" sound very similar just as they do in English. Jacob would never forget this river experience since it was here his own name was changed. Second, "crossing" over was also symbolic of what was about to happen. He was not only "crossing over" in terms of geographical movement, but he was "crossing over" into a new realm spiritually. He was leaving the old behind—his "name" and all that it symbolized in his past life—and moving ahead by faith, never to return to the river Jabbok.

We can only speculate what was in Jacob's mind at that moment. Clearly, he was still very frightened. Though details are sketchy, one thing is clear. Jacob was moving ahead with his plans to meet Esau. His move across the river was in the direction of Canaan. He was not retreating but forging ahead to remain true to the words he had given his servants to relay to Esau: "Your servant Jacob is coming behind us" (32:20).

## A Surprise Attack

Once Jacob had moved everything across the river, he remained behind on the other side. Alone—and in the darkness of the night—he was suddenly attacked by a "man" who engaged him in a wrestling match. Since Jacob was already frightened, we can only imagine the intense fear that gripped his soul. Though accustomed to being on guard against enemy attacks at night while shepherding Laban's flocks over the years, this experience was totally unexpected.

### No Ordinary Wrestling Match

This was no ordinary fight. It lasted "till daybreak" (32:24). Though the night must have been well along when he encountered this stranger, it was a long and desperate struggle.

Jacob held on tenaciously. He wouldn't give up. Neither could the stranger overpower him. Consequently, he put a move on Jacob that injured his leg, literally dislocating his hip joint (32:25). Ironically, this maneuver takes us back to Jacob's birth when he grasped Esau's heel—the kind of sly hold one wrestler puts on another in order to take control.

### Was This Another Dream?

There are certain aspects in this biblical account that are difficult to understand. In fact, some Bible scholars try to explain what is described here by suggesting that it is not a literal experience. However, we're not told it was a dream—such as Jacob had at Bethel. Consequently, I personally see no justification to interpret this passage in this way. Neither is it an allegory—a mythical story to make a spiritual point. This was hand-to-hand combat, flesh against flesh, man against man.

### Come the Morning

As the sun began to send its morning rays over the horizon, the stranger wanted to terminate the struggle. "Let me go," he said, "for it is daybreak" (32:26). We can only conclude that this man didn't want Jacob to look at him. More specifically, he did not want Jacob to see his face. In actuality, he was protecting Jacob because of who he really was. Jacob was wrestling with God Himself! Because of His awesome holiness, no man has ever looked directly into the face of God and lived (Exod. 33:20).

Jacob's reaction to the stranger's request is surprising. He wouldn't let go. By now, he must have known this man in some mysterious way represented his God. This is obvious from his response: "I will not let you go unless you bless me" (Gen. 32:26b).

## Painful Memories

Why this request? Why wouldn't Jacob let go? Could it be that this encounter surfaced old memories, and Jacob's mind connected with his deceptive antics over twenty years before when he had deceived his father into giving him the blessing Isaac was planning to give to Esau. After all, at this moment, Esau was uppermost in Jacob's mind. He was obsessed with developing a plan that would appease his brother and seek his forgiveness. Could it be that Jacob realized for the first time that in order to be as fruitful as God wanted him to be, he would need to legitimately receive the promised blessings from God that previously he had secured deceitfully.

Whatever Jacob's thoughts, the stranger zeroed in on Jacob's *innermost struggle*—revealing the divine nature of this encounter. "What is your *name*?" the man asked. If Jacob was indeed mulling over what had happened twenty years before when he deceived his father and received the blessing in a surreptitious manner, he would have certainly recalled Esau's deafening cry: "Isn't he rightly named Jacob?" (27:36).

## A Shameful Moment

When the stranger asked Jacob's name, Jacob must have released his grip and fallen limp at the stranger's feet, whispering his own name in shame (32:27b). The physical battle was over—and so was the spiritual battle that was far more important than the wrestling match. For most of his life, Jacob had promoted his own agenda. He was self-centered and self-driven. He was used to making his own way in life, deceiving when necessary. He relied on his own strength—both psychologically and physically.

But God was preparing him for this moment. In Jacob's mind, he was facing a potential encounter with Esau that could literally mean death for him and his whole family. He was more humble and meek than he had ever been in his life. He was desperately trying to return to his homeland as God had directed—even if he had to call Esau his lord and be his servant. He was actually willing to give up his place in history to be at peace with his brother (32:4–5, 20).

## A New Name

It was during this moment of weakness, while Jacob was exerting all the human strength he could muster, that God brought him to his knees and changed his name. "Your name will no longer be *Jacob*, but *Israel*, because you have struggled with God and with men and have overcome" (32:28).

### God Was Speaking

What did God mean? First of all, the name Israel means "he struggles with God." By changing Jacob's name, the stranger was also identifying who *He* was! He was none other than God revealing Himself in human flesh. He was meeting Jacob in a way that he could understand and grasp His presence.

### The Struggle Was Over

Jacob certainly didn't win the battle *against* God, but he won the battle against his own flesh and human desires to do everything in his own strength. He gave up his old stubborn ways of doing things and allowed God to be his strength and source of wisdom. In doing so, he would also be victorious over men. At that moment, Jacob must have thought of the four hundred men who, in his mind, may have been bearing down upon him to punish him for his sins. God was telling Jacob the battle was over before it had begun. This must have been reassuring to Jacob.

### Ultimate Victory

The meaning of these words, however, had long range implications. Because Jacob had admitted his sins and weaknesses and had yielded his life to God, his and his sons' victories over "men" would be ongoing. Though the man Israel and his descendants would be scattered to the ends of the earth because of their disobedience, the Lord would never forget His people—the *nation* Israel. God's promise to Abraham would be literally fulfilled. The land of Canaan was the Israelites' by divine decree—and at some future moment, they would possess it and be victorious over their enemies.

## A Nation Once Again

We've seen the beginning of the literal fulfillment of this promise in our generation. For the first time in centuries, we've witnessed the reestablishment of the nation Israel. It happened in 1948 when the United Nations recognized Israel as an independent state. Though their neighbors have tried on several occasions to drive them into the sea and to destroy them, they've not been victorious.

This is not an accident. It is a fulfillment of God's promise to Abraham when He called him out of Ur of the Chaldeans and promised that he and his descendants would occupy the land of Canaan (Gen. 12:1–3). More specifically, it reflects God's promise to Jacob that night He changed his name to Israel.

## *The Face of God*

There is something even more significant that happened during the wrestling match by the river Jabbok. When Jacob asked the stranger to identify himself by name, he responded with a rhetorical question, as if to say, "I needn't tell you because you know in your heart who I am—and that's enough." Jacob *did* know the stranger's identity. After receiving a blessing, he named the place Peniel, which means "face of God." Jacob (or should we say Israel) elaborated on why he chose this name: "It is because I saw God face to face, and yet my life was spared" (32:30).

### "All Peoples on Earth Will Be Blessed"

Though shrouded in mystery, this dialogue takes on unusual meaning when we consider what God did when He sent Jesus Christ to be the "God-man." I'm convinced that Jacob met Jesus Christ that night. It was an Old Testament manifestation of the Son of God. It was a preview of what God would one day do for the world in order to fulfill the most important part of God's promise to Abraham—that "all peoples on earth" would "be blessed" through Him (Gen. 12:1–3b).

### A Glimpse of Things to Come

In Jacob's encounter that night, several things paralleled the future coming of Jesus Christ. God appeared as a man. In his human form, he identified with Jacob's humanity—and ours. He literally wrestled with Jacob, and though He could have put him to death with a word from His mouth, He voluntarily restrained Himself and limited His strength.

However, He did not give up His deity, for with a simple touch, He wounded Jacob by putting his hip out of joint.

This is a beautiful picture of what Paul described in Philippians when he said, "Your attitude should be the same as that of Christ Jesus: Who, being in very nature God, did not consider equality with God something to be grasped, but made himself nothing, taking the very nature of a servant, being made in human likeness. And being found in appearance as a man, he humbled himself and became obedient to death—even death on a cross!" (Phil. 2:5–8).

## A Painful Reminder

God touched Jacob both physically and spiritually. Thereafter he limped—a constant reminder of his tendency to take matters into his own hands and leave God out. However, Jacob was a different man internally. Though he first met God in a dream at Bethel—which began his personal relationship with his heavenly Father—he now walked more closely with God, depending on Him and understanding the Lord's unique and divine purpose in his life. Though he was still human and would fail the Lord—as we all do—he would never be the same again. Unfortunately for Jacob, because of his persistent stubborn and self-centered will, God had to "hurt him" in order to "help him" to become all that God wanted him to be. Jacob, of course, would never forget his personal encounter with God that night in Peniel. And all religious and God-fearing Jews, even to this day, remember what happened to Jacob by not eating "the tendon attached to the socket of the hip" (Gen. 32:32).

## Becoming God's Man Today

*Principles to Live By*

In every encounter with Jacob, we learn some powerful principles to guide us in our Christian lives.

*Principle 1. Once we meet God through Jesus Christ, our lives are destined for change.*

Jacob's first experience at Bethel takes us, once again, to Paul's letter to the Ephesians where we read that God "chose us in him before the creation of the world to be *holy and blameless in His sight*" (Eph. 1:4).

This does not mean that our holiness is simply God seeing us as perfect and sinless because of the perfect and sinless sacrifice of Jesus Christ. That's true—thank God—but our position or status in Christ is never separated in God's will from the way we live our lives once we become true believers. It's also true that we are saved by grace through faith and not by works (Eph. 2:8–9), but we're also "God's workmanship, created in Christ Jesus to do good works, which God prepared in advance for us to do" (Eph. 2:10). As Paul also wrote to Titus, our "knowledge of the truth . . . leads to godliness" (Titus 1:1).

### *Principle 2. God is longsuffering and patient with our growth process.*

Thankfully, God understands our human weaknesses. He knew us before we were born, and He knows everything about us since we were born. And He also knows everything about us since we were "born again"!

We must understand, however, that God's patience and longsuffering with our weaknesses is directly related to our knowledge of what is right and wrong and the capacities we have to respond to that knowledge. To deliberately follow fleshly desires and to make decisions that are out of His will is to set ourselves up for discipline, which leads to another principle that cannot be separated from God's longsuffering and patience with our weaknesses.

### *Principle 3. If we are truly God's children, our loving, heavenly Father will discipline us in order to conform us to His holy image.*

We've already encountered the principle of God's discipline in the study of Jacob's life. But it's worth repeating—primarily because God reminds us of this truth so often.

God *is* a loving heavenly Father. The author of Hebrews tells us that if we're not disciplined when we disobey Him, perhaps we "are illegitimate children and not true sons" (12:8).

We must not be hasty, however, in drawing the conclusion we're not saved. Because we've not been severely disciplined does not mean we're not true Christians. Neither does it mean God approves of what we're doing.

For Jacob, it took twenty years for God to finally bring him to the place of complete humility and commitment to following God's will.

During this period he tried to do things in his own strength. Though successful materially, he suffered through years of ill treatment, family tension, and both physical and psychological hardships. Unfortunately, Jacob was so self-centered and self-willed that God eventually had to hurt him in order to help him—a wound he bore the rest of his life.

## Does God Work This Way Today?

Does this mean God will discipline his children today as He did Jacob? First of all, we must remember that most physical illnesses are not inflicted by God because we're doing something sinful. Some of the most godly people I know suffer from human tragedies. Unfortunately, all of us can be victims of the presence of sin in the world. On the other hand, it seems that some of the most evil people in the world go through life unmaimed. Only God knows and understands why "bad things happen to good people."

But the fact remains that God does discipline His children when they deliberately disobey Him and walk out of His will on a continual basis. Personally, I don't wish to test God's grace to see how much I can get away with. Neither do I wish to pray "Lord, put my hip out of joint so I can remember to walk in your will!" Rather, I want to pray—"Lord, help me not to be a Jacob! Help me draw closer to You by obeying what You teach me in Your Word. Lord, help me to present my body to You as a living sacrifice. Help me not to be conformed to this world's system but to be transformed by the renewing of my mind so that I'll be able to test and prove what Your good, acceptable, and perfect will really is!" (Rom. 12:1–2).

### Personalizing These Principles

Use the following questions to reflect on your own life as a Christian.

1. What positive changes have I seen in my life since I became a Christian?

2. How has God demonstrated His longsuffering and patience toward me when I have failed Him?

3. In what ways has God disciplined me when I have persistently walked out of His will?

4. If God gave me a new name to conform to my new life in Christ, what would He call me?

## Set a Goal

As you reflect on the principles in this chapter, what goal do you need to set in order to conform your life more to the image of Jesus Christ? For example, you haven't experienced the changes in your life you know you should have since you've become a Christian.

_____

_____

_____

_____

## Memorize the Following Scripture

*Do not be anxious about anything, but in everything, by prayer and petition, with thanksgiving, present your requests to God. And the peace of God, which transcends all understanding, will guard your hearts and your minds in Christ Jesus.*
PHILIPPIANS 4:6–7

## Growing Together

The following questions are designed for small group discussion:

1. What changes does God expect to see in our lives when we become Christians?

   To answer this question, read together 1 Timothy 3:1–7. Point out that these are not just character qualities for a spiritual leader. They should actually be spiritual goals for every man who wants to become a mature Christian who reflects the life of Jesus Christ.[1]

2. Would you share with the group how God has demonstrated His longsuffering and patience toward you when you have persistently walked out of the will of God?

3. How has God disciplined you in order to bring you back into His will? How did this make you feel ultimately?

4. Why do some Christians seem to get by with persistent and flagrant sin while others are seemingly disciplined rather quickly?

5. In this study, we've seen that God changed Jacob's name to Israel. Look at Acts 4:36–37 where the apostles changed Joseph's name to

Barnabas. Why did they make this change? What lesson is there in this illustration for every man who wants to reflect the life of Jesus Christ?

Chapter 12

# Reconciliation and Forgiveness
### Read Genesis 33:1–20

$L$ewis B. Smedes in his book entitled *Forgive and Forget* states: "If you cannot free people from their wrongs and see them as the needy people they are, you enslave yourself to your own painful past, and fastening yourself to the past, you let your hate become your future."[1]

## A Modern-Day Miracle

While perusing a daily newspaper, I read about a woman and her two children who were abducted from a grocery store parking lot. She was raped, shot four times, and left for dead. Her two children, ages three and seven, were shot and killed. The abductors were convicted of murder. One is on death row; the other is serving eight consecutive life sentences. When interviewed, the woman said that she doesn't hate these two men and feels no anger toward them. She explained her attitude to having put herself in God's hands. This indeed is a modern-day miracle. Only God can enable us to forgive our enemies for this kind of terrible deed.

Forgiveness is essential for spiritual growth. This doesn't mean we forget the wrong someone has done to us. But it does mean we don't allow their wrongdoing to control us and make us bitter.

## A Painful Memory

For twenty years, Jacob and Esau had been out of harmony with each other. Though separated by hundreds of miles, the emotional pain from the tension that existed between them continued to linger. Even after Esau had forgiven his brother, Jacob continued to experience fear and anxiety since the problem still existed in his memory. Esau's plot to kill him was deeply impressed in the recesses of his mind.

But all of that was about to change. Unknown to Jacob, Esau was coming in peace. The four hundred men accompanying him were simply attendants, not an army bent on wiping out Jacob and his family and stealing all of his possessions.

## A Lingering Fear

We're not told how much time elapsed after Jacob's "face-to-face" encounter with God (Gen. 32:30) and the moment when he "looked up" and saw Esau "coming with his four hundred men" (33:1). Personally, I think it happened quickly—perhaps the very next morning when the sun came up and the "stranger" disappeared.

However, one thing is very clear in the biblical text. Jacob was still frightened. The Lord's reassuring words that he would "overcome" in his struggles with men (32:28) were evidently eclipsed by the fear he felt when he looked up and saw the size of Esau's entourage.

### A Plan of Action

Jacob wasted no time. He had already made some preliminary plans for this moment (32:7). He quickly arranged his family into groups. Out front, he placed the two maidservants, Bilhah and Zilpah, each with the two sons they had born Jacob. Standing with Bilhah were Dan and Naphtali, and standing next to Zilpah were Gad and Asher.

Next in line stood Leah with her six sons—Reuben, Simeon, Levi, Judah, Issachar, and Zebulun. Standing among these six boys—perhaps holding Leah's hand—was their sister, Dinah.

### Obvious Favoritism

Jacob placed Rachel and her only son, Joseph, in the rear. His favoritism was very apparent. Rachel was and always had been his first love. Even though Leah had borne him six sons and a daughter, he still favored Rachel. With the prospect of being a victim of Esau's wrath, he made it clear to everyone who he was most concerned about.

Imagine the intense emotional pain this plan caused Leah. She had lived with this kind of trauma most of her life. On the other hand, she may have anticipated it. After all, it was no secret that Jacob loved Rachel. But this life and death decision by Jacob would only add insult to injury. Her fear mixed with anger must have been overwhelming.

## *Jacob, You Rascal!*

At this moment, it's easy to become angry at Jacob. Where was his faith? After all, he had just met with God face-to-face. He had received a special blessing. The Lord had told him he was going to overcome in his struggle with men. Furthermore, Jacob was limping—a reminder that God had to hurt him in order to get his attention. He even had a new name! Why couldn't he trust God now! Why would he put his family through this pain by showing such obvious favoritism?

It's easy to become judgmental of others when viewing their predicament from an enlightened position. Think about your own life. How quickly we can all slip back into doing things our way, even allowing old feelings to take control. After all, Jacob lived with his own pain for twenty years. He didn't ask for Leah! Having children through the two maidservants was not his idea. He cooperated because of the jealousy and competitive antics between Rachel and Leah. In his own mind, he probably felt justified with his plan. After all, he was about to step out and take the lead. He would be the first to lay down his life. They were all in this together, but just in case . . . !

If Jacob had trusted God as he should have, he would have gone out to meet Esau all by himself, leaving his family behind. He wouldn't have put Leah, Bilhah, Zilpah, and all their children through this kind of emotional pain. The ten sons would never forget this horrendous experience. It could very well have been the roots of their intense hatred towards Joseph that eventually caused them to sell him as a slave into Egypt (37:4).

Though I believe Jacob made a very bad judgment call regarding his family, we must not lose sight of the fact that he "went on ahead and bowed down to the ground seven times as he approached his brother" (33:3). This was ancient court protocol when subjects approached a lord or king. Jacob was definitely putting himself in a subservient role. Uppermost in his mind was the event that triggered Esau's anger twenty years before—the day he deceived their father and stole the blessing from his older brother. Though Jacob knew in his heart he was God's choice in fulfilling God's covenant with his grandfather, Abraham, he also knew *what* he did and the *way* he did it was sinful and wrong. In fact, it appears that he was actually willing to give up this role in order to be at peace with his brother.

## Is This an "Old Trick"?

Some believe Jacob was still up to his old tricks—in this case trying to manipulate Esau—and playing on his sympathy. In other words, some believe he was demonstrating subservience only because he knew his "back was up against the wall."

Personally, I think Jacob was very sincere and truly sorry for his actions—that his heart was right. Though he found it easy to regress to old patterns of behavior—as we've just seen by the way he showed favoritism—it doesn't mean that he wasn't sincerely attempting to right what he did wrong and to do the will of God. Clearly he was a different man, a man with a new name. Though he was not the man he should be or could be, he was not the man he used to be.

## A Striking Contrast

The contrast between Jacob's behavior and Esau's response jumps off the page in the biblical account. The moment Esau recognized Jacob, he ran to meet him. We read that he "embraced him; he threw his arms around his neck and kissed him" (33:4). Standing arm in arm, they both wept tears of joy and relief.

### Tears of Joy

Esau's tears were certainly more focused on emotional elation. He had no fear of Jacob, only a desire to see him and to be reconciled. We're not told when he had consciously and deliberately forgiven Jacob, but it could have happened years before. Even Rebekah, their mother, thought Esau would get over his anger rather quickly. That's why she told Jacob to leave "for a while" until Esau cooled off. "When your brother is no longer angry with you and forgets what you did to him," Rebekah reassured Jacob, "I'll send word for you to come back from there" (27:44–45).

From this statement by Rebekah, it appears that Esau was the kind of man who lost his temper quickly but also would cool off quickly. Jacob, on the other hand, was the kind of man who couldn't understand this kind of mentality. Had someone done to him what he had done to

Esau, he'd have probably carried the grudge for years and sought to get even.

But remember that Jacob had not received any word from his mother to return—as she had promised. Does this mean Esau allowed this wedge to linger much longer than she had anticipated? This question had to be in Jacob's mind as he went out to meet Esau. What a relief to be hugged rather than pierced through with a sword or dropped dead with arrows and spears from Esau's four hundred men.

## Tears of Relief

Jacob's tears, then, were probably tears of relief more so than tears of joy—though I'm sure he experienced both emotions. After all, he'd spent a number of horrible days worrying about the outcome of meeting his brother. He was convinced in his own mind that Esau was still angry and had amassed the four hundred men to retaliate. It was a matter of life and death, and only mercy could save Jacob and his family.

Imagine the sense of emotional release Jacob felt as he stood there arm in arm with Esau. Most of us cannot identify with these emotions. We've never deliberately walked into a situation that we actually believed could have resulted in a massacre. But most of us have experienced moments of incredible relief when we've anticipated that something bad was about to happen and suddenly it passed us by. By multiplying the intensity of this experience many times, we can only imagine the emotional release Jacob felt when he discovered Esau had come in peace. His emotions exploded with tears.

## *Esau's Sincerity*

Esau demonstrated his sincerity by immediately inquiring about Jacob's family. "'Who are these with you?' he asked. Jacob answered, 'They are the children God has graciously given your servant'" (33:5–6).

### "Who Are These with You?"

The next event must have been an incredible sight—and a tender moment for both Esau and Jacob. The two maidservants and their four sons approached Esau and bowed down before him. Next, Leah and her seven children did the same. Finally, here came Rachel and Joseph, also bowing before this often-talked-about uncle. Esau's heart would have been deeply touched as he walked among them, asking their names, shaking their hands, and patting the young ones on the head. We must remember that one-on-one reconciliation usually affects other people too. In this case, it involved a whole clan.

## "Why All These Animals?"

Esau next turned his attention to the 550 animals—the goats, the sheep, the camels, the cattle, and the donkeys—that he had met on the way. Again, Esau revealed his sincerity when he asked, "What do you mean by all these droves I met?" (33:8).

Jacob was honest in his response. He told Esau he was attempting to pacify him and "to find favor" in his eyes (33:8). Esau's response again demonstrated the reality of his own forgiveness. He told Jacob he already had plenty of animals. He tried to convince Jacob to keep them.

## *A Heart-Touching Speech*

Jacob responded with a heart-touching speech that persuaded Esau to keep the gift: "'No please!' said Jacob. 'If I have found favor in your eyes, accept this gift from me. For to see your face is like seeing the face of God, now that you have received me favorably. Please accept the present that was brought to you, for God has been gracious to me and I have all I need'" (33:10–11).

### Spiritual Memories

Inherent in this little speech is a very significant and revealing statement. For Jacob to meet Esau face-to-face and experience his forgiveness was "like seeing the face of God" (33:10). Spiritual memories must have flooded Jacob's mind:

- ➤ His experience with God's grace at Bethel when he was running from Esau (28:10–22).
- ➤ His protection when God appeared to Laban in a dream and told him not to harm Jacob when he was fleeing from his uncle (31:24).
- ➤ His encounter with the angels of God when he and Laban separated (32:1–2).
- ➤ His specific prayer for deliverance from Esau (32:9–12).
- ➤ And most importantly, his "face-to-face" encounter with God, perhaps the very night before he met Esau and experienced his brother's forgiveness (32:22–32).

## A Flesh and Blood "Reminder"

Jacob understood as never before God's grace and forgiveness in his life. Experiencing Esau's forgiveness became a face-to-face, flesh-and-blood reminder of what God had done for him all along when he was wandering in his own wilderness of sin and disobedience. Consequently, experiencing Esau's forgiveness was "like seeing the face of God."

## Jacob's Vow

There's also another very important insight that emerges from this little speech. When God revealed Himself at Bethel, Jacob was so overwhelmed with God's presence that he built an altar to the Lord and made a vow. We read: "If God will be with me and will watch over me on this journey I am taking and will give me food to eat and clothes to wear so that I return safely to my father's house, then the Lord will be my God. This stone that I have set up as a pillar will be God's house, and of all that you give me I will give you a tenth" (28:20–22).

## A Gift to Esau—A Gift to God

At the moment Jacob experienced Esau's forgiveness, he was certainly reminded of the way God had blessed him materially. His livestock had multiplied again and again. In fact, the Lord had given him divine wisdom in breeding. But Jacob also would have remembered his vow to give God a tenth of his possessions.

Though I cannot prove it from this text, I would not be at all surprised if Jacob's herd totaled 5,500 animals and the 550 he gave Esau represented 10 percent of his total assets. Here was a unique opportunity to fulfill his vow. After all, Esau's face was "like the face of God." He recognized that his brother's loving reactions were because of God's grace, not because of his own schemes and plans. Consequently, Jacob viewed this gift to Esau as an opportunity to give a gift to God. In other words, this was not just an exercise in soothing his conscience but an opportunity for Jacob to experience divine worship and thanksgiving with the material blessings that God had given him.

## *The Rest of the Story*

### Esau's Gracious Offer

The rest of the story moves quickly. Esau offered to accompany Jacob back to Seir where he lived. But Jacob graciously declined the offer, expressing concern particularly for his children and the young livestock that were nursing. He encouraged Esau to go on ahead and he'd follow at a slower pace (33:12–14).

## Jacob's Hidden Agenda

For some unstated reason, it seems Jacob never intended to go to Seir. Perhaps he felt it would be better to leave well enough alone. He and Esau were reconciled, and maybe he didn't want to take a chance on opening old wounds by living in the same community. This may have been his intent when he declined Esau's offer to at least leave some of his men to accompany him (33:15a). "But why do that?" Jacob asked. "Just let me find favor in the eyes of my lord" (33:15b). In other words, just experiencing Esau's ongoing forgiveness was enough.

## Why Not "Shoot Straight"?

Why did Jacob lie to Esau? Why didn't he simply discuss his intentions openly, perhaps even laying out his concerns that to live together in the same area might lead to some future conflict (if indeed this was Jacob's fear).

Frankly, when I first observed what Jacob did, I was very disappointed. Since God had so specifically protected him during this whole ordeal, wouldn't He protect him if he told Esau the whole truth, even if he hurt his brother's feelings? Again, from our vantage point, this seems so foolish, so ridiculous, so deceptive! And it is!

However, how often do we twist the truth because we're fearful of another person's reactions? To avoid conflict—or future conflict—we simply avoid raising issues that may erupt into something greater. We're particularly susceptible to this possibility when there has been a long history of tension, as there was between Jacob and Esau.

## Stepping over the Line!

Understanding Jacob's fears, however, doesn't justify his actions. Don't misunderstand! I'm not saying we must always reveal everything we're thinking and feeling. In these situations, we must—as Jesus said—be as wise as serpents and harmless as doves. However, God wants us to practice this principle without being dishonest. There is a line we shouldn't step over—and frequently it's our fear of conflict or rejection that causes us to step over that line. Jacob stepped over that line!

## Esau Was No Fool!

Some believe that Esau read between the lines anyway. Frankly, I'm convinced he did. In his heart, he knew that Jacob was not going to follow him to Seir.

How true that is of most people who know us well. They too can read between the lines, and they know when we're not shooting straight. How much more respect we'll gain if we simply tell the truth in a sensitive, honest way, expressing openly our fears about the matter without pointing our finger at the other party. In my experience, most people respond positively and sympathetically to this approach.

## "El Elohe Israel"

Jacob followed through on his "hidden" agenda. He and his family went to Succoth rather than to Seir. There he settled down in the land of Canaan. He "built a place for himself and made shelters for his livestock" (33:17). Furthermore, like his father, Abraham, he built an altar to the Lord. Jacob named this altar El Elohe Israel (33:20). In essence, Jacob was saying, "The God of Israel is an 'El'"—that is, a strong God, a mighty One, a God who keeps His promises. Jacob was back in the land, and he wanted everyone to know it was the God of his fathers who brought him safely back.

### Becoming God's Man Today

*Principles to Live By*

Fear is a normal emotion that can cause us to do things we'd ordinarily not do, even under the best of circumstances. Again, Jacob demonstrated very poor judgment by showing favoritism and later distorting the truth. Consequently, we must constantly be on guard against this "old flesh pattern." Jacob's weaknesses teach us how easily we can regress to old sinful behaviors.

And there are several other principles that emerge from this particular moment in Jacob's life story.

*Principle 1. We should seek forgiveness from those we've sinned against.*

Jesus made this point very clear in what has come to be called the Sermon on the Mount: "Therefore, if you are offering your gift at the altar and there remember that your brother has something against you, leave your gift there in front of the altar. First go and be reconciled to your brother; then come and offer your gift" (Matt. 5:23–24).

In this passage, the focus is clearly on the one who has offended a fellow Christian. This means that before we proceed to do anything—including offering our gifts and worship to God—we should ask forgiveness if we've sinned against another brother or sister in Christ. We should not let another day go by without at least making plans to do something about it.

Once we've asked forgiveness, it's up to the other person to forgive. If they do not, the problem rests with them. We have cleared our own conscience. We have done what God has asked. The challenge for each of us is to make sure we have offered a sincere and heartfelt apology.

### Principle 2. We should seek to be reconciled with those who have sinned against us.

Again, Jesus made this point clear in a very explicit passage of Scripture: "If your brother sins against you, go and show him his fault, just between the two of you. If he listens to you, you have won your brother over. But if he will not listen, take one or two others along, so that 'every matter may be established by the testimony of two or three witnesses.' If he refuses to listen to them, tell it to the church; and if he refuses to listen even to the church, treat him as you would a pagan or a tax collector" (Matt. 18:15–17).

The focus in this passage is on one who has sinned against us as individuals. The sin is not against the body of Christ collectively, but it's a personal offense. In that case, we are to take four steps.

*First*, we are to approach that person and share the offense. Jesus made clear that we are to go alone, although in some instances this may have to be by telephone or by letter.

*Second*, if the person will not listen to us and we want to pursue the situation in order to achieve reconciliation, we should take one or two others with us.

*Third*, if the person still will not listen and be reconciled, then we can take it to a higher authority. In this passage, Jesus used the term "church" or assembly. This can be the elders or spiritual leaders in our church.

*Fourth*, if this person refuses to listen even to those in authority in the church, then we are to treat this individual as a non-Christian.

It's at this point that we often misunderstand what Jesus meant. Personally, I believe that Jesus was teaching that we should forgive the person as Jesus forgave His enemies when He hung on the cross. We should not continue to hold a grudge. We should simply relate to them as if they're unbelievers who are trapped in their own sins. We should pray for them and trust God to bring them to the place where they can experience God's forgiveness in Jesus Christ.

### Principle 3. We should seek to restore people who are trapped in sin.

The apostle Paul clarified this principle when he wrote to the Galatians: "Brothers, if someone is caught in a sin, you who are spiritual should restore him gently. But watch yourself, or you also may be tempted. Carry each other's burdens, and in this way you will fulfill the law of Christ" (Gal. 6:1–2).

The focus in this passage of Scripture is clearly on an individual who has sinned not against you personally but against the Lord Jesus and the body of Christ. This is a person who is trapped in some sin—such as an alcoholic, a sex addict, an adulterer, or an abuser. The challenge here is to those "who are spiritual." Note that this calls for more than one individual to restore this person. This is a task for several people. This is not a personal offense. Consequently, more than one person should be involved right from the beginning. That's why Paul used the plural pronoun *you*. In fact, it can be dangerous to approach this kind of person alone. They may lie and distort the truth, actually accusing you falsely without a witness to protect you.

Notice also that you are to attempt to restore this person. This should be an effort at helping a person to confess his sin in order to be set free. It is not initially an effort at breaking fellowship and separating yourself from that person. It involves attempting to bring this person back into the fold.

Note also that this is to be done "gently" or "humbly." We are not to approach this kind of situation with arrogance or pride. We must realize that we too can be tempted—even caught in the very same sin. This is also why more than one person should be involved in this kind of intervention.

### Principle 4. We should do everything we can to live in harmony with our brothers and sisters in Jesus Christ.

This is what Jesus taught His disciples in the Upper Room: "A new command I give you: Love one another. As I have loved you, so you must love one another. By this all men will know that you are my disciples, if you love one another" (John 13:34–35).

The apostle Paul called love the greatest virtue of all (1 Cor. 13:13). We are to pursue love, and love means maintaining unity.

This is also what Jesus prayed for. In this sense, love and unity are inseparable concepts: "My prayer is not for them alone. I pray also for those who will believe in me through their message, that all of them may be one, Father, just as you are in me and I am in you. . . . May they be brought to complete unity to let the world know that you sent me and have loved them even as you have loved me" (John 17:20–21, 23).

King David once wrote, "How good and pleasant it is when brothers live together in unity!" (Ps. 133:1). And, Paul stated that we are to "make every effort to keep the unity of the Spirit through the bond of peace" (Eph. 4:3).

## Personalizing These Principles

The following questions will help you apply these principles to your life. Answer them as honestly as you can.

1. Is there someone I have sinned against whom I have not asked for their forgiveness? What step should I take immediately?

2. Is there someone who has sinned against me, and I have not been able to be free from that offense? Seek wisdom from another mature brother in Christ as to how to resolve this problem.

3. Do I know someone who is trapped in sin who needs restoration? Consult with your pastor or some other mature brothers regarding how to proceed.

4. Am I doing everything I possibly can to maintain love and unity in my marriage, family, and local church? What should I do to bring about this unity?

### Set a Goal

As you review these principles, which one stands out as a point of action for you? Set a goal to do something about it as soon as possible. If you have difficulty discerning whether or not you should take action—and what you should do specifically, seek wisdom from another mature member of the body of Jesus Christ:

_____
_____
_____
_____
_____

## *Memorize the Following Scripture*

> *How good and pleasant it is when brothers live together in unity!*
> PSALM 133:1

## *Growing Together*

The following questions are designed for small-group discussion:

1. Would you feel free to share a way in which you have dealt with the subject of forgiveness and reconciliation?

2. What have you learned about this process in your own life?

3. What should we do when a person will not forgive us? How can we handle this situation?

4. What specific area in your own life would you like for us to pray about?

## Chapter 13

# Back Home Again
### Read Genesis 35:1–15

*I*n the late 1960s and early 1970s multiple thousands of young people bought into the "new morality" that promoted drugs, sexual promiscuity, and free speech. This eventually gave birth to the Jesus movement—particularly on the college campuses where the "new" lifestyle had taken its painful toll. I personally witnessed a multitude of disillusioned youth respond to the gospel message, realizing they had bought into a lifestyle that led them down a path that in some instances literally led to destruction. One song that became popular among Christian young people had a beautiful message of invitation to those who were turning to Christ. It was simply called "Welcome Back!"

In many respects, this was God's message to Jacob after many years of difficulty and disillusionment working for his Uncle Laban. In our final lesson on Jacob, the Lord "welcomed him back to Bethel," the place where he first met God more than twenty years before. As stated earlier, I believe this is when Jacob experienced personal salvation and redemption.

## Partial Obedience

When Jacob was still in Paddan Aram, God spoke to him one day and told him to return to the land of his fathers and his relatives (Gen. 31:3a). Jacob responded. He began the journey homeward and God protected him—just as He said He would (31:3b). However, Jacob's obedience was partial. He decided to settle in Shechem. Perhaps Jacob reasoned that he was at least across the border and in Canaan. After all, he was out from under his Uncle Laban's cruel control, he was at peace with Esau, and from a human point of view, Shechem certainly seemed a good place to settle down.

## The Truth Hurts

Though Jacob's reasoning seemed to be logical, it lacked one important thing—God's perspective. As far as we know, Jacob didn't even consult God about this location. Had he done so, God would have certainly reminded him of what He had told him earlier—to "go back to the land of your *fathers and to your relatives*" (31:3). Perhaps Jacob remembered only too well what the Lord had said earlier and didn't care to raise the question lest he get an answer contrary to what he really wanted to hear.

How true that is of so many of us today! When we want to do something we already know is out of the will of God—or at least out of harmony with divine principles—we often avoid consulting God. We conveniently stop reading the Scriptures and praying. Some of us even stop going to church because what we hear makes us terribly uncomfortable. We already know what God has said, and we don't want to be reminded. However, when we do walk out of His will, we always end up in trouble. And that's exactly what happened to Jacob.

## *Dinah's Moral Failure*

When Jacob and his family settled in Shechem, a sad thing happened to Leah's daughter, Dinah. She "went out to visit the women of the land" (34:1). We must remember that the Shechemites were pagans. Their values were diametrically opposed to God's moral and spiritual laws. We can speculate that these women introduced Dinah to Shechem, the ruler of the city that was named after him. Noting that she was a beautiful woman, the Scriptures record that he took her and "violated her" (34:2). In other words, he probably seduced her and then convinced her she should stay with him. It's doubtful he forced her against her will. Rather, she was probably enamored with Shechem's lavish lifestyle and all he could offer her. After all, he was a prince.

When Dinah's big brothers heard about what had happened, they were livid. However, their moment came when Shechem wanted to marry their sister. Ironically, his "lust" turned to "love." We read that "his heart was drawn to Dinah . . . , and he loved the girl and spoke tenderly to her" (34:3).

## Cruel Revenge

Jacob's sons used this change of heart as an opportunity to avenge their sister. They immediately devised a very deceptive and cruel plot. Sadly, two of the brothers—Simeon and Levi—took matters into their own hands and murdered every adult male in the city. They also looted the city, carrying off "all their wealth and all their women and children, taking as plunder everything in the houses" (34:29).

When Jacob heard what had happened, he was terribly frightened. He knew that the other Canaanites in the area would join together and retaliate. From a human point of view, there was no way Jacob and his family could survive this kind of warfare since they were "few in number" compared with their enemies (34:30).

## *More Grace*

Once again, God was faithful to Jacob. Even though he had failed to obey God completely and return to his father's home, God spoke to him and told him to move on to Bethel. Had Jacob consulted the Lord, he would have gotten this message much earlier and circumvented all the problems that were created in Shechem. But like many of us, it takes a crisis to keep us seeking God and walking in His perfect will. This was the story of Jacob's life!

## It's Easy to Forget

God was reminding Jacob of the dream he'd had at Bethel and the vow he had made twenty years before. At that time, Jacob was filled with fear and cried out, "How awesome is this place!" (28:17). He then made a promise to God—a vow we've looked at several times before, but which bears repeating again: "Then Jacob made a vow, saying, 'If God will be with me and will watch over me on this journey I am taking and will give me food to eat and clothes to wear so that I return safely to my father's house, then the Lord will be my God. This stone that I have set up as a pillar will be God's house, and of all that you give me I will give you a tenth'" (28:20–22).

Clearly, God had done His part. He had watched over Jacob—time and again—delivering him from both his uncle, Laban, and his brother,

Esau. He had provided him with food to eat and clothes to wear. In fact, he had multiplied his flocks many times.

However, Jacob had not done his part completely! He had not returned to "his father's house"—though he had moved in that direction. Though Jacob had acknowledged God and had prayed to the Lord—particularly when he was in trouble—he had not been consistent in his faith.

### The Great Shema

Jacob's most important omission is that he had not led everyone in his family to forsake the gods of Mesopotamia. He had yet to help his family commit totally to the truth that "God is one" and there are no other gods.

This great truth is foundational in Hebrew and Christian theology. This is why Moses emphasized this point when he reviewed the Law for Israel, just prior to their entrance into the Promised Land. "Hear, O Israel!" he cried. "The Lord our God, the Lord is One" (Deut. 6:4). Known in Israel as the "Great Shema," this truth pervades the darkness of paganism like a beacon that permeates the blackness of a starless night, warning sailors of the rocky shoals that await them if they pursue their present course.

Not only had Jacob failed to teach his household this foundational truth, but when God provided him with the opportunity, he had not done his part by fulfilling his promise to worship and praise God at Bethel. Furthermore, even though he may have given a tenth of his material possessions to Esau, he still needed to honor his vow to give a tenth to God—a significant part of his promise to worship the Lord at Bethel!

## No Ifs, Ands, or Buts

When God spoke to Jacob this time, there is no evidence that Jacob hesitated. He knew what God was asking and he remembered what he had promised the Lord at Bethel. God didn't have to spell it out. He had to break all his associations with idolatry and separate himself completely from pagan deities. He could not worship God as the one true God while his family dabbled in witchcraft, mysterious magic, and bowing down to "household gods." Furthermore, he could not fulfill his vow by staying in Shechem.

## An Unwavering Command

To this point we have not seen Jacob take strong and direct leadership in his family. He had been "walking on eggshells," not knowing what kind of emotional outbursts he would face from Leah and Rachel. He had experienced enough of those in Paddan Aram to last a lifetime. Consequently, he had probably honed the fine art of diplomacy, knowing that there would be no peace or rest without compromise.

However, things changed. Jacob was *very* direct when he said, "Get rid of the foreign gods you have with you, and purify yourselves and change your clothes" (Gen. 35:2). Finally, Jacob was in control of his household.

## No Exceptions!

Jacob directed his orders at his whole family—his wives, their maidservants, his twelve children—and all of the servants he had acquired in Paddan Aram. Being the patriarch of the family, he had the authority to issue this order, and anyone who didn't acquiesce would have been in serious trouble.

I don't think anyone in Jacob's household resisted and grumbled. Everyone had seen God's miraculous hand in delivering them from Laban's wrath. They had also observed God's intervention with Esau. And they knew at this moment they were in danger of massive retaliation for the mass murder that had just taken place in Shechem. I'm convinced they were waiting for Jacob to take control and be the leader he should have been all along.

## What About Rachel?

At this point, it's appropriate to ask what happened to Laban's gods. The last we knew, Rachel had stolen them, packed them in her traveling case, and was sitting on them, giving her father the impression she couldn't move because she was menstruating (31:30–35). Did Rachel keep these "gods"? If so, where were they? What did she do with them?

Though I have no specific biblical facts, I believe Rachel still had these gods and used them. We must remember that even though her own father was a member of Abraham's extended family, she still lived in an idolatrous environment. Laban also worshipped these false gods. The fact that Abraham eventually turned from idols to serve the one true God in no way means the rest of his pagan family followed suit. In fact, God called him to leave his family and their false gods—not to try to lead them out of idolatry. After all, Abraham himself was not personally converted until a number of years after he left Ur.

It follows then that most of Jacob's family probably still dabbled in their pagan religions. To complicate matters, Jacob had not been a strong witness to his wives and children, let alone his servants. Even though he had come to know the one true God, he had been living a very carnal life during most of his stay in Paddan Aram. Though it must have been difficult for Jacob, he had to address this issue with Rachel as well. More than we realize, she may have been a negative witness to the rest of Jacob's household.

## Let's Get Specific!

Jacob's directive to all his household was not only straightforward and unequivocal but also very specific (35:2). Everyone was to remove *all* of the foreign gods—no matter what form they took. They were to "purify" themselves—probably to literally bathe, an external symbol of becoming "internally" clean. And they were to put on clean clothes—another symbol to demonstrate a whole new way of living.

Jacob next outlined *where* they were going—and *why*! Obviously, as stated earlier, Jacob's whole household knew about Bethel. Though they didn't understand the depth of what had happened there, they knew Jacob had had a unique experience with his God. So Jacob now made it very clear that he was returning to Bethel to "build an altar *to* God"—not *a* god. He reported that this was the God who had answered him in his distress—which fills us in on a very important detail that is not mentioned in the original Bethel event (28:10–22).

## A Light Came On

Jacob had prayed for help while he was running from Esau, and God had heard him. He wanted everyone in his household to know that it was this God—the God of Abraham and Isaac—who had been with him wherever he had gone following the Bethel experience. At this point, Jacob was telling them something they had probably never heard before. Twenty years before, he had made God a promise in his prayer for protection on the journey that lay before him, namely, that he would worship God at Bethel on his return to his father's house. It's almost as if the light had suddenly dawned in his own heart: God had done His part—but he had not done his!

## Sound Familiar?

It's amazing how we can get so bogged down in our own world that we fail to see God's providential hand in our lives. Sometimes this goes on for years—until we suddenly face a crisis that brings us face-to-face with God's will for our lives. Suddenly, we see our selfish way of life and recognize that in spite of our egocentric behavior, God has been faithfully by our side, just waiting for us to recognize His presence! This happened to Jacob as a result of his Shechem experience.

## On the Move Again

Everyone in Jacob's household was well aware of what had just happened in Shechem. Their company now included a number of other people—the wives and children of the men Simeon and Levi had murdered! Imagine the consternation and confusion this created!

### A Life-Threatening Experience

To add to their emotional turmoil and fear, a number of clans in the area were no doubt already joining forces in order to attack Jacob. If that happened, every male would be fair game, especially since Simeon and Levi had wiped out every man in Shechem. Furthermore, they knew the tide would be reversed—that all of *their* women and children would be taken captive and made slaves. To say the least, everyone in Jacob's household was in the mood to listen and respond to his command.

Pragmatically, they all knew time was of the essence. They could be attacked at any moment. But Jacob's sincere witness regarding the God of Bethel must have touched their hearts. Though their motives for obedience may have been somewhat mixed, they "gave Jacob all the foreign gods they had and the rings in their ears." Jacob, in turn, "buried them under the oak at Shechem" (35:4).

### Was This True Repentance?

Apparently a number of people in Jacob's household had an array of gods, including other sacred ornaments. Among these ornaments were earrings that were worn by both men and women. They were considered magical and were worn for "divine protection." Think for a moment about what was happening. They actually turned these "protective" ornaments over to Jacob in the midst of impending doom.

In the New Testament, this kind of attitude and action is described as "repentance"—changing one's mind and heart in turning from a false view of God to a right view. In this Old Testament setting, it appears that most of these people sincerely transferred their allegiance from faith in false gods to faith in the one true God. Note, too, that Jacob buried everything they gave him, signifying they were gone forever. I believe this is a beautiful Old Testament picture of New Testament conversion when people repent, turn from their sins to Jesus Christ, and are baptized to demonstrate that they have died with Christ and have been raised to a new life.

## God's Protection

Once Jacob's household had packed all their belongings, loaded their camels, and corralled all their livestock, they headed off for Bethel. Once again, God honored their obedience with supernatural protection. We read that "the terror of God fell upon the towns all around them so that no one pursued them" (35:5). God was clearly demonstrating that they needed only Him for divine guidance and protection—not the false gods and other assorted religious paraphernalia that they had brought with them from Paddan Aram.

## *Full Circle*

When Jacob and his household arrived in Bethel, in many respects he had come full circle. It was here he first met God personally, and now he was back to fulfill his vow. He immediately "built an altar, and he called the place El Bethel." Previously, he had simply named this spot Bethel, which means "house of God." He now modified that name to El Bethel, which means "God of Bethel." He made this change "because it was there that God revealed himself to him when he was fleeing from his brother" (35:7).

## Why This Change?

This second experience at Bethel took on far greater meaning for Jacob. Years of difficulty and pain, successes and failures, praying and forgetting to pray—all of these experiences had taught Jacob many spiritual lessons. Most of all, God had become much more personal.

The recent crisis in Shechem—which definitely got Jacob's attention—seems to be the point at which it dawned on Jacob in a new way how faithful God had been to him all these years. At this moment, Bethel was not just a place where he had met God but rather a place that reminded him of God's presence with him all these years, protecting and caring for him in spite of his weak faith and carnal lifestyle.

## A Public Announcement

Not only was Jacob's return to Bethel a new and deeper experience with God, but it was also where his name was formally changed to Israel. When he had wrestled with God in the form of a man at Jabbok, the Lord changed his name that night (32:28). However, it appears that God made this name change public at Bethel.

God also reviewed for Jacob the covenant He had made with his grandfather, Abraham, and his father, Isaac. He would become "a community of nations" (35:11). The land of Canaan was also his, just as it belonged to Abraham and Isaac (35:12).

Though Jacob did not fully understand all that God was saying—and particularly the way his descendants would bless the whole world—he now understood more fully than ever before his place in God's providential plan. He also knew he had received God's blessing in God's way—not through deceit and manipulation.

Jacob was clearly a different man. After having built an altar, he also "set up a stone pillar at the place where God had talked with him." To express his love and commitment to God, he poured out a drink offering on the pillar and poured oil on it (35:14).

## Home Again

As important as Bethel was in Jacob's life, it was still just a stopping-off point—a place to worship God. Eventually, he moved on again, and now he was known as "Israel" (35:21–22). Eventually, he arrived in Hebron, where he was reunited with his father who had now reached the ripe old age of 180. How ironic! Isaac thought he was about to die years before when he promised to give Esau his blessing and was deceived by his wife, Rebekah, and his son, Jacob (27:2–4).

Imagine the warmth this brought to this old man's heart. Though he couldn't see Jacob, he could touch him—this time knowing he was touching not a man posing as his eldest son, but a man who now walked with God.

## Isaac's Death

Shortly after Jacob had returned home, Isaac "breathed his last and died." The Scriptures simply read he was "old and full of years" when he went on to meet those who had gone before. But jumping off the page are these words: "Esau and Jacob buried him" (35:29). Two brothers who were at each other's throats now joined together to lay their ancient father to rest.

## The Curtain Falls

At this point, the curtain falls on Jacob's life story. There's more, of course, we can learn about his life, but we'll not meet him again until we study the life of his beloved son, Joseph.

## Becoming God's Man Today

*Principles to Live By*

We've already touched on several important truths that can be gleaned from this final study in Jacob's life. But let's formalize these truths into principles.

*Principle 1. It's easy to make decisions that are based on environmental and emotional factors rather than on what God says His specific will is for our lives.*

This is what happened to Jacob when he settled in Shechem. He was out from under Laban's suffocating control and manipulation. He had been united with Esau. And he was back in the land. However, he either forgot or ignored the fact that God had told him to return to his "father's house." Most of us have fallen prey to this same kind of decision making. But, don't misunderstand. Environmental factors *are* important in determining the will of God. And how we feel about things is also important. However, there must be one overriding factor in determining the will of God—what God actually says! This is where we must begin in determining what God wants us to do. Nothing must contradict God's divine instructions in the Word of God. Therefore, anytime we are making a decision, we must ask ourselves whether or not we are violating the direct Word and will of God.

God gives us great freedom in making our decisions. But He also gives us important guidelines in the Scriptures. For example, we can choose our partners in business or marriage, but we are never to be unequally yoked with unbelievers in a way that will bring tension into our lives that leads us to compromise other aspects of God's will (2 Cor. 6:14–18).

Remember also that when Jacob settled in Shechem, he subjected his family to a very worldly environment. He miscalculated the impact it would have on his family. Consequently, he paid a terrible price when Dinah fell prey to Shechem's sinful ways.

It's true that we cannot remove ourselves from the world's system. We have no choice but to "live in it," but we must make every effort not to become "a part of it." Unfortunately, some Christians make decisions to live too close to the world, the flesh, and the devil! Look what happened to Lot and his family when he chose to ignore God's warnings and settled in Sodom and Gomorrah.

In our culture, we bring the influence of the world into our living rooms and bedrooms by television. No wonder our children fall prey to sinful influences. For example, a steady diet of MTV can destroy any young person's moral resistance. Though we cannot remove ourselves from the world, we can make decisions that will minimize its influence.

*Principle 2. Partial obedience will eventually lead to crises that result in heartache and even disaster.*

In Jacob's case, his daughter became influenced by the world and allowed herself to be seduced. As a result, his sons committed mass murder. Consequently, what started out to be a very pleasant experience after years of turmoil in Paddan Aram turned out to be a horrible nightmare!

Fortunately, most of our decisions that are not based on complete obedience to God's will do not result in this kind of disaster. However, "partial obedience" of any kind will eventually lead to some very difficult experiences and heartbreaking situations. We cannot straddle the fence and be at peace. There is only one safe and secure place for the Christian: in the center of God's "good, pleasing and perfect will" (Rom. 12:2).

*Principle 3. Complete obedience means ridding ourselves of anything that can be classified as "a foreign god."*

In preparing this material, I asked a group of men and women I pray with weekly to list the various "foreign gods" Christians sometimes have in their homes today. Interestingly, almost 100 percent of this group immediately thought of television.

Does this mean Christians should take their TV sets out in the backyard and bury them? Not at all! But if you can't control it, if it has a grip on your heart that you can't break, you'd better do something to rid yourself of this "foreign god!" Otherwise, it will master you and you will eventually pay the consequences. But, let's get even more specific. What about the "god" the Bible calls materialism? Are you worshipping this "foreign god?" Let me help you answer this question:

➤ Do you have cable television or a satellite dish? How much does it cost each month? Do you tithe, that is, give 10 percent of your money to the Lord? "Oh, I can't," you say. "I can't make ends meet if I give that much to the Lord's work." If the money you spend on cable or satellite TV is keeping you from giving to the Lord as you should, is that not a "foreign god?"

➤ What about your car? What kind is it? Understandably, transportation is important in our culture. It's part of our economic way of life. But are the payments on your luxury car keeping you from giving as you should to the Lord? Could you not drive a less expensive car, get the same service, meet your economic needs, and then be able to give as you should to the Lord? Don't misunderstand. I'm not suggesting that driving a luxury car is wrong. But if your luxury car keeps you from giving what you should to God, is that not a "foreign god"?

➤ What about the home you live in and the way you've furnished it? Now again, please don't misunderstand! We all need a roof over our head. And it's not wrong to have nice things and to live comfortably. But are you living a lifestyle that keeps you from giving regularly and proportionally to God? Could you not have a safe and secure place to live and at the same time have money left over to give to the Lord? If living beyond our means keeps us from giving to God on a regular and proportional basis, is that not a "foreign god"?

## Personalizing These Principles

Use the following questions to help you evaluate your Christian life.

1. Am I doing anything that is in violation of what God says is His perfect will for my life?

   Consider the following exhortations from Paul's letter to the Ephesians. Use them as a criteria for evaluating your own lifestyle.

☐ "Each of you must put off falsehood and speak truthfully to his neighbor" (4:25).

☐ "In your anger, do not sin. Do not let the sun go down while you are still angry, and do not give the devil a foothold" (4:26–27).

☐ "He who has been stealing must steal no longer, but must work, doing something useful with his own hands, that he may have something to share with those in need" (4:28).

☐ "Do not let any unwholesome talk come out of your mouths, but only what is helpful for building others up according to their needs, that it may benefit those who listen" (4:29).

☐ "And do not grieve the Holy Spirit of God, with whom you were sealed for the day of redemption" (4:30).

☐ "Get rid of all bitterness, rage and anger, brawling and slander, along with every form of malice" (4:31).

☐ "Be kind and compassionate to one another, forgiving each other, just as in Christ God forgave you" (4:32).

☐ "Be imitators of God, therefore, as dearly loved children and live a life of love, just as Christ loved us and gave himself up for us as a fragrant offering and sacrifice to God" (5:1–2).

☐ "But among you there must not be even a hint of sexual immorality, or of any kind of impurity, or greed, because these are improper for God's holy people" (5:3).

☐ "Nor should there be obscenity, foolish talk or coarse joking, which are out of place, but rather thanksgiving" (5:4).

2. Am I rationalizing my decisions and actions by telling myself I'm obeying God fully, when in reality it is not *complete obedience*?

3. Is there anything in my life that could be considered a "foreign" or a "household god;" namely, is there anything that keeps me from putting God first in my life in terms of my time, my talents, and my treasures?

## Set a Goal

As you reflect on the principles in this chapter, what do you need to do to give up a "foreign god"? For example, are you spending your money on what is a want and a luxury, not a need, while this expenditure is keeping you from giving generously to the Lord? Set a specific goal to get rid of that particular "pagan god":

_____

_____

_____

_____

_____

## Memorize the Following Scripture

*Do not love the world or anything in the world. If anyone loves the world, the love of the Father is not in him. For everything in the world—the cravings of sinful man, the lust of his eyes and the boasting of what he has and does—comes not from the Father but from the world.*

1 JOHN 2:15–16

## Growing Together

The following questions are designed for small-group discussion:

1. Why is it easy for men (and women) in American culture to avoid living in complete obedience to God?

2. How much of our disobedience is based on ignorance? How much of it is simply ignoring what we know God wants us to do?

3. What kind of a crisis have you experienced (or seen someone else experience) because you've only been partially obedient to God?

4. As you've studied Jacob's experience, have you isolated a "foreign god" in your own life? Would you feel free to share what that "god" is and what you plan to do to get rid of it?

5. What are some things we can pray specifically for you?

# Endnotes

## Chapter 1

1. C. F. Keil and F. Delitzsch, *Commentary on the Old Testament*, The Pentateuch (Grand Rapids: Wm. B. Eerdmans Publishing Co., 1980), 1: 268.

2. For further information, see Alan P. Ross, *Creation and Blessing* (Grand Rapids: Baker Book House, 1988), 440–41.

## Chapter 2

1. Some commentators believe that only the adjective *godless* applies to Esau. However, others believe both adjectives—*godless* and *immoral*—describe Jacob's brother. Personally, I favor the second interpretation based on the Greek construction as well as Jewish tradition, which at the time Hebrews was written depicted Esau as an "immoral" man.

## Chapter 3

1. Abraham's faith must have been bolstered at this moment by his experience with the angels who appeared to him "near the great trees of Mamre" (Gen. 18:1). These angelic beings who appeared as men delivered Lot and his family from Sodom. Once again, Abraham knew that God would fulfill His promise even if He had to accompany Eliezer in the form of an angel.

2. Charles F. Pfeiffer and Howard F. Vos, *The Wycliffe Historical Geography of Bible Lands* (Chicago: Moody Press, 1967), 2–3.

3. The meaning of the Hebrew for the word *meditate* isn't certain. It could mean to pray or simply to think.

## Chapter 4

1. Ross, *Creation and Blessing,* 471.

2. Though the following texts are laid out in dramatic form, the Scriptures are taken directly from the NIV text. However, a few adaptations are made in order to maintain the flow in this new format. For example, phrases such as the following are omitted: "And said to him;" "he answered;" "Isaac said;" etc.

3. Two examples of "lying" that appear justifiable in God's sight are when Rahab saved Joshua's surveillance team from death by hiding them on her rooftop and telling the inhabitants of Jericho that they had already left (Josh. 2:4–5). Another example is when the Hebrew midwives saved the newborn Hebrew boys from death by falsifying to the King of Egypt what actually happened. In this instance, God blessed these women for what they did (Exod. 1:15–21). We must be very careful, however, in utilizing these examples to justify "situational ethics." Rationalization can easily set in because of our sinful hearts. Our motives can be clearly selfish rather than pure and noble as the examples we've just sighted.

## Chapter 5

1. Ross, *Creation and Blessing,* 489.

2. John recorded several of these events in his gospel (Nicodemus, the woman at the well, etc.).

3. Ross, *Creation and Blessing,* 492.

4. Ibid.

## Chapter 6

1. Marrying within the family structure was not considered a problem in Jacob's culture. No doubt Cain, son of Adam and Eve, married a sister in order to launch the human race. In this case, Rachel was Jacob's cousin.

2. Keil and Delitzsch, *Commentary on the Old Testament*, 285.

## Chapter 9

1. These three names appear together eighteen times in the Pentateuch, two times in the rest of the Old Testament, five times in the Gospels, and three times in the Book of Acts—a total of twenty-eight times in Scripture (Gen. 50:24; Exod. 2:24; 3:6,15–16; 4:5; 6:3, 8; 33:1; Lev. 26:42; Num. 32:11; Deut. 1:8; 6:10; 9:5, 27; 29:13; 30:20; 34:4; 2 Kings 13:23; Jer. 33:26; Matt. 8:11; 22:32; Mark 12:26; Luke 13:28; 20:37; Acts 3:13; 7:8, 32).

2. This chronology is based on the assumption that God's revelation to Jacob in 31:13 came before the revelation in 31:3. This assumption is explained in the previous chapter.

## Chapter 11

1. For an in-depth study of these character qualities, see Gene A. Getz, *The Measure of a Man* (Ventura, Calif.: Regal Books, 1995). This volume was completely rewritten and released in a new format.

## Chapter 12

1. Lewis B. Smedes, *Forgive and Forget: Healing the Hurts We Don't Deserve* (San Francisco: Harper & Row, 1984), 29.